'Like a great painting, God's plan of redemption deserves both close inspection and 'big picture' analysis from a distance. Using an ingenious method, the author provides both, through more general and more detailed views of each subject he raises. Part C. S. Lewis, part John Stott, Simon Austen in this work both invites conversation with unbelievers and offers an eminently accessible theology course for mature believers and new Christians. Wherever the reader is on the spectrum, this book will reinvigorate as it informs, delight as it challenges, and fill both heart and mind with wonder that God has in fact bothered with us more that we know.'
Dr Mike Horton, Westminster Theological Seminary California

"Shrewd, sane and sensible, I wish this book every success. By success I mean that those who at present don't bother with God will read it and discover that God bothers with them".
Rev Dick Lucas, Rector Emeritus, St. Helen's Bishopsgate

"How wonderful to have a book that both sets out and defends the Christian faith - whilst helping the reader get a clear perspective of the past, the present and the future. As the title suggests, it makes it very clear why God should bother with us. This is an accessible, engaging and comprehensive explanation of the C̶̶̶̶̶̶ ̶̶̶̶̶̶̶̶ ̶̶̶̶̶̶̶̶ ̶̶̶̶̶̶ recommend."
Rev Rico Tice, All

SIMON_AUSTEN

WHY_SHOULD GOD_BOTHER WITH_ME?

CHRISTIANITY_FRESHLY_EXPLORED

CHRISTIAN_FOCUS_PUBLICATIONS

ISBN 1-85792-719-2

© Simon Austen 2002

Published in 2002
by
Christian Focus Publications, Ltd.
Geanies House, Fearn, Tain,
Ross-shire, IV20 1TW, Great Britain

www.christianfocus.com

Printed and bound by Cox & Wyman, Reading

Cover Design by Alister MacInnes

CONTENTS

INTRODUCTION   7

PART_ONE — WHAT_HAVE_I_DONE?

1. GOD_AND_CREATION   13
2. MANKIND_IN_REBELLION   41
3. MANKIND_UNDER_JUDGMENT   67

PART_TWO — WHAT_HAS_GOD DONE?

4. JESUS   89
5. THE_RESURRECTION_AND_THE_CHURCH   129
6. A_NEW_HEAVEN_AND_A_NEW_EARTH   161

PART THREE — WHAT NOW?   181

NOTES   185

INTRODUCTION

A short while ago I was speaking with a man who had recently become a Christian. As most of his friends did not share his faith in Jesus I asked him what they would read in order to help them understand what the Christian faith was all about. His reply was direct and simple. 'They don't read,' he said. 'Magazines and newspapers, yes. Books, no.'

It is perhaps ironic then that I have chosen to write a book with the hope that those who don't usually read might find it useful. To that end each chapter is divided into three sections. The first section of each chapter looks at the basic truths of Christianity. It is brief, concise and to the point. The second explains those truths a little more fully. The third seeks to provide something of an answer to the questions often asked when the Christian faith is explained. The book can be read in a matter of minutes by simply looking at the first sections of each chapter (in large print), or it can be studied over a longer time by reading sections two and three.

I hope it proves a useful tool for the Christian as well as a stimulating read for those who do not understand the Christian faith. Inevitably a book of this size cannot cover everything, but it may be enough to stimulate further enquiry. Use it critically. Do not stop searching until you have found a satisfactory answer to the question 'Why should God bother with me?'

PART_I

WHAT_HAVE_I DONE?

1

GOD_AND
CREATION

GOD_AND
CREATION

I

The Christian message begins with God. The Bible tells us that he is the creator of the universe and its rightful ruler. He created the world from nothing. First he made the 'stage' – the land and sea and sky. Then he made 'the players' – animals of all sorts to inhabit the earth. The pinnacle of his creation was mankind, made in his image, to be in relationship with him and to be responsible for the rest of creation.

At the outset, all relationships were perfect. Mankind lived in loving obedience to God, mankind lived in a loving relationship with one another and mankind lived in harmony with the created order. We are told that God looked at all that he had made and said that it was 'very good.' So the picture we have is one of perfection, with all that God made living under his authority.

GOD_AND
CREATION

II

It might surprise us to discover that in the early twenty-first century many people claim to believe in God. Figures vary, but the consensus seems to be at about 70 per cent Atheism, as an alternative, does not appeal to many. The attempt to leave God behind in the wake of scientific advancement has raised as many questions as it has answered. In the last one hundred years we have seen two world wars, one of which included the barbaric destruction of six million Jews; we have seen a technological explosion and with it unparalleled pollution; we have greater powers of communication than ever before and yet we see gross inequality and a breakdown of marriage and family relationships. In the confusion many are left asking if there is more to life.

In 1992 Henry Grunwald, the former editor-in chief of *Time* Magazine and Ambassador to Austria, wrote an essay entitled 'The Year 2000: Is it the end – Or just the beginning?'[1] His observations resonate with the experience and questions of many:

> We are beset by a whole range of discontents and confusions. For a great many, the dunghill has become a natural habitat. . . . One of the most remarkable things about the twentieth century, more than technological progress and physical violence, has been the deconstruction of man (and woman). We are seeing a reaction to that phenomenon. Our view of man obviously depends on our view of God . . . . The ultimate irony, or perhaps tragedy, is that secularism has not led to humanism. We have gradually dissolved – deconstructed – the human being into a bundle of reflexes, impulses, neuroses, nerve endings. The great religious heresy used to be making man the measure of all things; but we have come close to making man the measure of nothing.

Perhaps it is for that reason that so many 'alternative' and pre-Christian 'beliefs' have emerged and taken hold in recent years. The humanists may not have got it right. Somehow, despite all the attempts to do away with God, there remains a hope that there is more to life, that life itself is not simply an accident of nature but fuelled with intent and design. Despite all the advances in medicine and science, the increase in comfort and prosperity, there is a hole inside us, a hole which longs to be filled — a hole not satisfied by so much of the secular materialism of our time and culture. Bernard Levin, the famous columnist, wrote:

> Countries like ours are full of people who have all the material comforts they desire, together with such non-material blessings as a happy family, and yet lead lives of quiet, and at times noisy, desperation, understanding that there is a hole inside them and that however much food and drink they pour into it, however many motor cars and television sets they stuff it with, however many well balanced children and loyal friends they parade around the edges of it ... it aches.[2]

So at the beginning of the twenty-first century God remains a real option, even a desire and hope in the modern mind. Indeed, some of us have even admitted to needing God. Douglas Coupland, in *Life after God*, expresses the thoughts of many:

> Now here is my secret: I tell you with an openness of heart that I doubt I shall ever achieve again . . . my secret is that I need God — that I am sick and can no longer make it alone. I need God to help me give, because I no longer seem capable of giving; to help me to be kind, as I no longer seem capable of kindness;

to help me to love as I no longer seem capable of being able to love.[3]

The need has been admitted, intellectually and personally. We need God. And yet as we seek to find out who God is and what he is like, we are confronted by a host of alternative and competing claims. The current mindset might encourage us to think of God in terms of 'what he means to you' but it will not wash. It is too dangerous. If I am at liberty to define God, then I will allow him to sanction whatever I choose, however selfish. He will abide by my rules, not I by his. He will sanction my selfishness, agree to my neglect of others, accept my level of morality and behaviour. No, we must allow God to tell us what he is like. We must seek to discover how he has revealed himself to us. And for the Christian that revelation in scripture is clear. You may have questions about scripture (which we shall address later), but as we look at the Bible it is possible to answer the question 'What is God like?' At this stage, three answers will suffice.

He_is_an_Almighty_Creator

When I have spoken to people about God, their first question has often been to do with science and creation. It is an important topic – and the third section of this chapter deals with it – but it can also be an unimportant topic; unimportant because it can cloud the real issue. We so often get bogged down with the 'how?' when the question the Bible encourages us to ask is 'who?' and 'why?'

> 'To whom will you compare me?
> Or who is my equal' says the Holy One.
> 'Lift your eyes and look to the heavens; who created
> all these?
> He who brings out the starry host one by one, and
> calls them each by name.
> Because of his great power and mighty strength not
> one of them is missing.'[4]

The fact that God created the universe is taken for granted in the scriptures. We may know more than the ancient mind in terms of science but the reality of the universe is no less amazing. In some ways our increased knowledge makes it that much more amazing. 1977 saw the launch of the Voyager 1 space probe. It was to travel through the solar system at 38 500 miles per hour. Even at that speed it would take 70 000 years to reach our solar system's nearest neighbour, Proxima Centauri – a concept which our finite minds have great difficulty in handling. And yet the claim of scripture is that God created the universe by the word of his mouth. What is more, the scriptures claim that you and I, as human beings, were designed in his image, as the pinnacle of his creation. He gave humanity the capacity to love and be loved, just like him; he gave men and women the role of being his vice-regents in the world he had created, to look after it, to enjoy its beauty, in perfect harmony with the creator and the created. It is a picture of perfection and intimacy. God is an almighty creator.

HE_IS_A_HOLY_JUDGE

We all long for justice. But justice cannot be administered without judgment. And for judgment to be right and fair it depends on three factors: The integrity of the judge, the purity of the law, and the appropriateness of the sentence.

THE_INTEGRITY_OF_THE_JUDGE

Imagine for a moment that your house was broken into, or your car stolen. The police get to work quickly and within a few weeks you find yourself in court, watching, listening, as the criminal faces the judge. The case is heard and the judge pronounces the sentence. 'Guilty.' You breathe a sigh of relief. Justice has been done. But then the judge continues... 'You have done something wrong and you have been found guilty. But I am a loving judge, a kind judge, a forgiving judge. I will let you off. You are free to go.'

If that really happened you would be outraged. The man on trial was found guilty. He clearly was in the wrong. How can that judge simply let him go? Kind and forgiving it might be — but just? No!

I expect that all of us would react in the same way and rightly so. We long for justice to be done. And yet at the same time we long for God to behave differently. We can cope with the notion that he is loving and forgiving but justice and judgment get a bad press. It causes us to feel rather uncomfortable or to wonder how the notion of judgment can square with a God who is meant to be forgiving. It's not that we want God to be free of judgment — we want him to judge

Hitler, or Saddam Hussein, or the man who stole our car, or the boy who bullied our son, or the man who cheated on his wife. It's just that we don't want him to judge *us* – to judge *me*. And so we subtly, almost imperceptibly, shift the goal posts. *We* decide what is right and wrong, who is 'in' and who is 'out,' who should go to heaven and who should not. And invariably, as we subtly shift those goal posts, we put ourselves on the right side of wrong, hoping, even assuming, that God will turn a blind eye to our wrongdoings – that our slight cheating of the tax man is acceptable, that our lustful thoughts are not really as bad as all that, that we are really quite decent folk after all. Surely God will forgive us – after all he is a loving and forgiving God!

But how is that different from our courtroom scene, with a judge who lets off the man who broke into our house? The only difference is that *we* have decided what is right and wrong, good and bad. Such decisions have been the feature of humanity from Genesis 3 (as we shall go on to see) and far from being just, the concept is riddled with injustice. Someone who is 'better' than us will draw the line of acceptability somewhere else, in a position where he will become acceptable, but we might be rejected.

Or what about the person 'below' us in the pecking order – the one who had fiddled their tax forms more, or had more lustful thoughts? The line of acceptability, or acceptance before God that we draw will exclude them. In fact any line we draw other than that of absolute perfection will be flawed and unfair. It will always include some and exclude others, leaving those excluded crying 'am I not good enough?'

What we need are perfect standards from a perfect judge. A judge like God, who, as we are told in the Bible 'will judge the world in righteousness, and the peoples in his truth'[5]

The_purity_of_the_law

I hope the need for a just judge, a judge with integrity, has become clear. As we read the scriptures we see a God, the creator God, who is perfectly just and fair. He is what the Bible calls 'holy'. It is this holy God who set out his standards, or to pick up our earlier analogy, who has drawn his line of right and wrong.

Increasingly few of us are familiar with the Ten Commandments, which are part of the 'law' that God gave to his people thousands of years ago. But even many of those familiar with their content and commands miss what they are all about. We can so happily, perhaps confidently, say that we keep the Ten Commandments, that we live by them. After all, we have never stolen anything, we have never murdered, we have never committed adultery. But the first commandment simply states 'You shall have no other gods before me.'[6] God requires us to put him first in all things, to love him totally with all our being, to live as we were designed to live, in perfect harmony with him and with those around us. That is his 'standard,' the line which he draws. And as we stop and think, as we look into our hearts, our diaries (which often dictate what our priorities are in life), and our bank accounts, then our heads drop. No, we haven't kept his standards. They seem too lofty, too impossible, too unreal, too perfect . . .

Yet what else would we expect from a holy perfect God? He must be perfect to be perfectly just. But if he is perfectly just then inevitably my injustice is highlighted all the more. And as we grasp that truth, as we begin to see what we are really like before this holy God, so we will begin to see what Christianity is all about.

THE_APPROPRIATENESS_OF_THE_SENTENCE

Occasionally injustice hits the headlines – someone has been released from prison having been pardoned, or someone hasn't had a fair hearing or has been wrongly accused for a crime they didn't commit. We all hate injustice. Any casual study of how children interact with one another will demonstrate how the concerns for justice run very deep within us.

We all understand the inherent rightness of an appropriate sentence for a particular crime. And when it comes to God, it is the same. He would be neither just nor loving if he let us off in the name of forgiveness. His love drives him to be forgiving, as we shall see, but never at the expense of justice. The sentence we receive is just. We should expect nothing less from a perfect God.

HE_IS_A_LOVING_FATHER

At the heart of our God there is love and there is relationship. The whole Bible reveals God to be a God of love who seeks to enter into relationship with people. He made mankind to be in relationship with him – to enjoy his company and his creation, to be in fellowship with him. Again and again God's

love and care are demonstrated in the Bible. But they are
seen most clearly and perfectly in the coming of Jesus into
the world. Speaking of Jesus, John (a disciple of Jesus) wrote:

> He came to that which was his own, but his own did
> not receive him. Yet to all who received him, to those
> who believed in his name, he gave the right to become
> children of God — children born not of natural descent,
> nor of human decision, or a husband's will, but born
> of God.[7]

It is possible not just to know about this God, but to know him
personally, as a son to a father. Perhaps that doesn't seem
much of a shock or surprise to us. Many of us are brought up
calling God 'father, and the word 'God' has not lost its
greatness, but somehow we have failed to realise just what
that means. When the footballer Eric Cantona returned to the
football league after being banned for kicking a spectator, he
hit the front page of *The Times*. One supporter was asked why
he had paid £80 for a ticket on the black market. 'Because
God is playing at Old Trafford,' he replied. A similar incident
occurred during the British Lions rugby tour of South Africa in
the summer of 1997. The Lions won the first test of a series
of three. They went on to win the series by a victory in the
second match. Just before the kick-off a commentator
interviewed the captain, Martin Johnson — the large crowd
behind him audible to the television viewers. 'Martin,' he
said 'You are ninety minutes away from being God.' Thousands
of viewers knew he was talking about greatness. But that is

where it stops. We fail to realize just how great God is, but we also fail to realize that we can actually know that God as our Father.

Other religions have many names for God — Islam has ninety-nine, Hinduism has more than a thousand, but neither can call God 'Father'. The Christian has the privilege of calling him 'my Father.' Remember what John said about Jesus? 'Yet to all who received him, to those who believed in his name, he gave the right to become children of God — children born not of natural descent, nor of human decision or a husband's will, but born of God.'

I sometimes look out at the stars when the night is clear. Before me is a vast array of space. It makes me feel insignificant. But the Bible tells me that the one who created all this — and is the rightful Lord of heaven and earth — has also created me. I may have rebelled against him, I may have ignored him and done my own thing, I may only give him any time when I am in need or on Christmas day, I may be deserving of his just judgment; but his love means that I can know him as Father, and I can be adopted as his child. What a shock, what a privilege.

We have seen in this section that God is the almighty creator, he is the holy judge and he is the loving Father. He is the rightful ruler of the world because he made it — and he is the rightful Lord of my life because he made me. But his Lordship and my response to it don't add up. There remains a mighty gulf between this great God and me. A gulf I have no hope of crossing on my own.

GOD_AND
CREATION

III

HASN'T_SCIENCE_DISPROVED
CHRISTIANITY?

It is almost impossible to come to the subject of God and creation without raising the issue of science. For the last hundred years or so, science has been used as the final nail in God's coffin, held up as the ultimate proof that all we read in the Bible is wrong. Only now is the mindset breaking down as the world discovers that while we may indulge in the benefits science has brought we are still left with a world beset by the confusion and inequality of the prescientific age.

Many of us pick up the debate which raged in the middle of the nineteenth century and which polarized the issue into those who accept a literal six day creation (and therefore reject all scientific theory) and those who accept scientific theory (and therefore reject the Genesis account). I will not pretend that the argument is simple or that it can be dealt with adequately in these few pages, but we can at least make a start.

In order to make sense both of Genesis and scientific theory we need to remove a few boulders of presupposition and deal with the textual evidence and scientific evidence presented to us.

SCIENCE — FRIEND_OR_FOE?

It is commonly thought that science and Christianity are mutually exclusive — one being to do with faith and not fact, the other fact and not faith. Whilst at first sight this may be the case, a closer examination of the two reveals much more common ground than one might initially think. Indeed, were it not for Christianity, science may never have got off the ground. From the sixteenth century onwards science developed in a Christian context:

> The concept of strict and generally valid laws of nature could hardly have arisen without the Christian concept of creation.[8]

> The Biblical doctrine . . . provides a more stable, rather than a less stable   foundation for our normal scientific expectations.[9]

Gradually science came to be a more acceptable way of explaining the world. The creation story was ridiculed by many and consequently people sought to reinterpret a traditional six day creation in the light of newly emerging theories. The wedge between science and Christianity was in place, a wedge which has fuelled agnosticism and atheism to this day, but a wedge made more of paper than solid science or theology.

Science has in so many ways prospered and served mankind. We live in a less painful and more comfortable world in which we can communicate easily – all because of science. Its advances have made the world a better place in which to live. And we accept science and scientific theory because it makes the best sense of the observed data, of the information available. As more information is available, so scientific theories have to be modified, consolidated or abandoned. What we are taught at school and what we read in books are simply the best models to fit the observable facts. As we accept them we are trusting them to be correct, and usually find that they work in practice. Of course there are many things which we don't know and can't answer – our knowledge and understanding are limited both by the vocabulary we have constructed to describe the events and the minds we use to interpret them. For example, we commonly accept that the universe goes on 'forever,' but we will never be able to visualize or understand what 'forever' means. Our minds can only deal with the finite. Likewise at the other end of the scale we cannot comprehend the infinitesimally small. Even the smallest particles known to man are made up of other

particles, which in turn are made up from other particles...
and so on. Every scientific discovery begs a further question.
The quest becomes inexhaustible. We cannot hope to
comprehend such extremes – our knowledge is really quite
minimal and only operates in a limited band of 'reality'. Science
makes sense of that reality and gives us enough certainty to
begin to make sense of that which is beyond that band of reality.

When it comes to the Christian faith, we are on remarkably
similar ground. We cannot fully comprehend the extent of God
and eternity; such ideas are in many ways 'beyond' us. But
there is a point at which God has made himself knowable, a
point at which he touches the understandable realm – the
realm also occupied by science. The person of Jesus Christ is
that point. His life, death and resurrection are rooted in history,
reasonable and historically reliable. Faith in Jesus rests on
more solid ground than at first we might imagine – something
that the writer of the letter to the Hebrews (a letter in the
New Testament) knew only too well: 'Faith is being sure of
what we hope for and certain of what we do not see'. Belief in
Jesus Christ is reasonable. His life, death, and supremely his
resurrection stand up to scrutiny.

Of course, not everything is easy to understand and some
questions in the realm of faith are difficult to answer, but
there is enough to be sure, enough to say that the Christian
faith is not empty hope but reasonable belief. So with science.
We know enough to make sense of that which we do not know.
Even if, for the sake of argument, personal encounter with
God is put to one side, there is still enough 'objective evidence'
to say that Christianity is true.

When it comes to our major stumbling block, namely scientific theory relating to the origins of the world, we are in an unusual position. As with the resurrection, evolution cannot be repeated. We cannot go back millions of years to show that the theory works in practice. Point mutation is more certain, that is small molecular changes in the DNA (the body's encoded material for construction), which brings about small changes within the organism; and similarities can be found between the DNA of similar species (such as apes and humans). But beyond that we cannot be certain about evolutionary theory. It is a very good explanation of the facts that we have, but it can never be more than a theory. Likely though it is, it can never be repeated. Even the oft-cited Darwin realized the limitations of his theory:

> Darwin himself considered that the idea of evolution is unsatisfactory unless the mechanism can be explained. I agree, but since no one has explained to my satisfaction how evolution could happen, I do not feel impelled to say that it happened. I prefer to say that on this matter our information is inadequate . . . There is a great divergence of opinion among biologists, not only about the causes of evolution but even about the central process. This divergence exists because the evidence is so unsatisfactory and does not permit certain conclusions.[10]

And whilst evolution remains for many a more likely explanation than a literal six day creation, it is still a very open field of research:

> Evolution . . . is scientific precisely because it is continually subject to modification and disproof in the light of fresh insights and data accrued in numerous fields of research.[11]

Even when one assumes the plausibility of evolution, the notion that the world is as it is and we are as we are because of a mere chemical accident or freak mutation is very hard for most people to accept. Many non-Christians marvel and ponder at the power behind the emergence of life. Indeed, our experience of order and design suggests that there is someone or something behind it all. We should not be so naive as to say that what we see *must* have a creator behind it, but equally, we shouldn't be surprised if there is!

> The idea that life was put together by random shuffling of constituent molecules can be shown to be as ridiculous and improbable as the proposition that a tornado blowing through a junk yard may assemble a Boeing 747. The aircraft had a creator, so might life.[12]

The probability of random molecules coming together in such a way as to produce the self replicating basis of life (DNA) has been compared to the likelihood of reconstructing the Oxford Dictionary by cutting up its constituent words and throwing them up into the air only to find that they have landed in alphabetical order. Of course, it is *possible*, but when one adds to that possibility the numerous other pointers to the authenticity of the Christian faith, the possible becomes increasingly remote.

Even if we assume that life occurred by random chance, we are still left with a higher, more complicated question — a question beyond the realms of science and beyond our comprehension — namely, from where did the constituent components come in the first place? How did the stage for this particular scientific play come into being? We have gone beyond science — and we still have no answers.

So science leaves us with probable scenarios, which seem likely but are unprovable. And after 150 years of debate and polarization, science has left us on the edge of our knowledge looking with philosophical uncertainty to what is beyond.

Two important considerations remain.

THE_TEXT_OF_GENESIS

One of the problems of the debate between Science and Christianity is that the majority of us engage neither with the Bible nor with science. For a start, the first few chapters of Genesis are answering different questions to the ones raised by science. The Bible was never designed to be a scientific text book. The whole aim of Genesis chapter one is not to tell us how the world was made so much as to tell us who made it. The main 'players' in the whole drama are God and mankind - and the Bible is all about that relationship; its formation, its destruction and most importantly, its recreation. A closer look at the text of Genesis will show us that the immediate rejection of God on the basis that the Bible is just ancient myth, will not satisfy. There is more to it than that.

For a start, twenty-first century presuppositions are very different from those prevalent in the second millennium before Christ, when the text of Genesis was probably written.

> Modern man makes assumptions about the world that are very different from those of the second millennium before Christ. Consequently, when we read Genesis we tend to grab hold of points that were of quite peripheral interest to the author of Genesis and we overlook the points that are fundamental.[13]

As a result of this 'overlooking of points' a variety of attempts have been made to massage scientific theory or the text of Genesis into a mutually compatible position, often with little success. The text is all we have and it is with the text that we must engage.

When Genesis was written there were a number of texts in circulation around the Ancient Near East (ANE) which dealt with similar stories (the creation of the world, the flood etc.) Consequently many have placed the text of Genesis in the same camp and written it off as ancient myth. But if we had been around at the time we would have been struck by how different the text is to any other known at the time. Unlike any other ANE material, Genesis makes it clear that the stars, the sun and the moon are not gods to be worshipped. On the contrary, it states clearly that the one and only God (the God of the Bible) made them. God is the Lord of his creation, and supremely the Lord of mankind. Humanity is therefore not seen to be the lackey or provider for the gods (as with other ancient material) but rather the pinnacle of God's creative activity.

As we look further, other differences emerge. The majority of ANE material sees the seventh day as a day of ill omen. Genesis sees it as a day of sanctity and blessing. Unlike other ANE material, there is not a collection of competing gods but one God who set the ordered structured universe in motion. The God who emerges from the first chapter of Genesis is holy and sovereign, the creator of the universe as seen.

But the real question that persists in the twenty-first century mind surely relates to the days themselves. Are we meant to believe in a literal six day creation in which each day is a twenty-four hour period? Some have sought to show that although the text envisages each day to be a twenty-four hour period (from the language used), it should be taken as the psalmist suggests 'For a thousand years in your sight are like a day that has just gone by.'[14] However, true as the Psalm might be, Genesis does not encourage us to think of each day as a representative period of time. A day in Genesis is more than likely a literal twenty-four hour period. That said, we must remember that 'The six day schema is not one of several means employed in this chapter to stress the system and order that has been built into creation.'[15]

There is also strong textual argument for assuming that the days are a literary device which function to make a theological point. A close inspection of the text will reveal that the luminaries (the sun and moon) were not made until day four, and yet were designed 'as signs to mark the seasons, *days* and years.'[16] In other words 'days' as we know them were not present until the fourth 'day' in the creation story — a remarkable concept if the author really wanted us to think of each day in literal terms.

In the second chapter of Genesis (v.5) we are told that 'no shrub had appeared and no plant had grown because the Lord had not yet sent rain on the earth.' Such a comment must presuppose the normal laws of nature where water is required for plants to grow. If we are expected to take the days of chapter one in a literal fashion, then either chapter two makes little sense or the stories are separate and incompatible. I doubt the latter. Although it might have been favoured by theologians down the years, those same theologians have proposed extensive editing of the Old (and New) Testaments. Such a glaring inconsistency would surely have been edited out if their proposals are correct!

It seems far better to hold the two chapters in harmony, to recognize that the text was not written with a twenty-first century scientific mindset and to remember that it is all about God, the sovereign creator, and mankind, the pinnacle of his creation.

Once we realize what Genesis is all about, the picture of a powerful creator God becomes clear. A God in perfect harmony with his perfect creation. A God who looked at all that he had made and saw that it was 'very good.'[17]

Only it doesn't ring true with our experience. Yes, we see great beauty in the world and in people, yet that same world is ugly and relationships (personal and corporate) can be messy. The good, the bad and the ugly all mixed up together. This book helps to explain why – and what God has done about it.

THE_FRUIT_OF_SCIENCE

There is no doubt that science has made many advances from which we all benefit. It is a great privilege to live in the West in the twenty-first century. We have sanitation, wonderful medical care, better education and communication; we live longer and have more leisure time. Our homes are warm and we are well fed. All because of science. And yet the utopian ideal associated with the onset of the scientific age has not manifested itself as its proponents might have hoped. We are better at killing people, because science has developed the ability for us to do so. We are sanitized from poverty, cocooned in comfort, while many people die from preventable diseases. The gap between rich and poor grows daily. The world's resources are being as exploited as are the people who occupy the world.

It is not that science is bad. It is us. We are the ones who use what is good in ways which so often prosper and benefit ourselves whilst ignoring the plight of others. There is something in human nature which means we cannot do what we should do; we cannot live in harmony with one another, with the world and with God. Something has gone terribly wrong. That something is what we shall be looking at in the next chapter.

2

MANKIND_IN
REBELLION

MANKIND_IN
REBELLION

1

As we look at the world today it is far from the picture of perfection that we were left with from Genesis chapter one. God had looked at all that he had made and it was 'very good'. We look at the world around us and it seems that what was good has been mixed with what is bad and ugly. The Bible explains why.

From the very beginning, men and women have rejected God. Rather than doing things his way, we have chosen to do things our way. Whether this rebellion takes the form of active rejection or simply ignoring him, the reality is that we choose to live our way rather than his. This is what the Bible calls 'sin.'

It is the consequence of this rebellion that has made the world what it is. Rather than seeking to serve him, we serve ourselves. Rather than living in harmony with one another, there is discord, strife, hatred, hurt, broken relationships. Rather than living in harmony with the created order, we see people struggling to grow food while others have too much, there are natural disasters and we exploit the planet.

We have rejected God's rightful rule of our lives. We have made ourselves into the 'lords' of all we do. The result is what we see around us. And all this stems from humanity's basic rejection of God.

MANKIND_IN
REBELLION

II

We don't have to look very far before we realize that the world is not as it was designed to be. If we look at all that God has made we might find it hard to say that it is 'very good.' There is no doubt that at times we will delight in the created world around us. As we lie on a sandy beach with the sound of the sea and the last rays of the day's sun warming our bodies and our hearts, we may well think how good the world is. As we experience the kindness and generosity of our friends and neighbours, we may well delight in the love of one to another.

Equally there are times when we see the horror of the world. We read history books and realize the terrible destruction of humanity which has marked the twentieth century. We read the newspapers and see the millions who starve and the thousands who suffer injustice. William Rees-Mogg began a recent article in *The Times* newspaper with these words:[18]

> The world is full of violence. There are massacres in East Timor; the murder of 300 Russians by terrorist bombs, probably related to Chechnya; the ethnic cleansing of the Albanians and then the Serbs in Kosovo; the Nato bombing itself, which has left Serbia devastated and Kosovo polluted with unexploded cluster bombs; the grumbling confrontation in Kashmir between India and Pakistan, both nuclear powers; Saddam Hussein's plans for weapons of mass destruction; the Anglo-American response of sanctions and bombs. However safe we may feel going about our usual business in one of the West's great cities, this century of violence is ending with worldwide violence, and the threat of worse to come.

And it is not just 'out there'. Our cars are stolen, our houses burgled. Our children are exposed to alcohol and drug abuse. Relationships break down. The gap between rich and poor seems to grow daily. In 1994 it was calculated that the wealth of the world's 387 billionaires equalled the combined wealth of the bottom 45 per cent of the entire world's population.[19] It is horrific, and yet we do so little about it. We happily spend money on things we don't need and we waste food – even *we* play our part in making the world what it is.

WHAT_WENT_WRONG?

The world now is certainly a different world to the one we read about at the beginning of the Bible. There everything was perfect – the world was a good place. God lived in harmony with mankind, man and woman lived in harmony with each other and with the created order. God's people lived in God's place and enjoyed God's blessings.

But as we have seen already, our experience of the world is very different. Something has gone horribly wrong. In Genesis chapters one and two the world was perfect. By Genesis chapter four the world was spoilt. There we find the first murder, we find loneliness and alienation. Genesis chapter three explains why.

Most of us have some knowledge of Genesis chapter three. Adam, Eve, the serpent and the apple have been the subject of many paintings, songs and jokes. It is all too easy to write it off as ancient myth – or at least to feel a little confused by it. If you have read the last section of the first chapter, you might be a little more cautious about ignoring the first few chapters of the Bible. They don't tell us about science – they were never designed to do so. But they do tell us about God, his world and what went wrong with it.

The Bible talks about the events of Genesis chapter three as real events but with symbolic elements. It is important for us to understand this chapter because it shows why things went wrong. It is an explanation of why the world is as it is. It explains how the 'very good' became what we see today – a world in which the good is mixed with the bad and the ugly.

Fundamentally the problem was that mankind, created to be in relationship with God, rebelled against God. There were three aspects to that rebellion, all of which we see in the world today.

MANKIND_DOUBTED_GOD'S_WORD

The garden of Eden was a wonderful place. It was a picture of perfection. Adam and Eve were free to enjoy its beauties and wonders, but they had to do so in obedience to God. The one instruction was this:

> And the Lord God commanded the man, 'You are free
> to eat from any tree in the garden; but you must not
> eat from the tree of the knowledge of good and evil,
> for when you eat of it you will surely die.'[20]

At first sight this instruction may sound mean and harsh. Surely it is a good thing to know the difference between good and evil? And if God is supposed to be a loving God, then why did he give any instructions at all? Let's try and answer those questions.

The problem wasn't simply to do with knowing what was good and knowing what was bad. Adam already *had to know* what was good and what was bad (in other words what he should and should not do) if he was to obey God's instruction. God had, in effect, told him that it was 'bad' to eat from this particular tree — *and he understood.* He already therefore had some knowledge of what was good and what was evil.

The real issue with this tree was not so much knowing what was good and evil, but deciding what was good and evil. God's concern was that man should not set himself up as God, that God alone should reserve the right to decide what was right and wrong. It is obvious really. If God is perfect, then inevitably his standards of right and wrong are also going to be perfect. Any alternative 'regime' or rule is unlikely to work. It is perhaps no surprise then that the world in which we now live is messy. There is injustice, hatred, fear, war etc. And why? Because mankind has rejected God and taken over the responsibility of deciding what is right and wrong – with disastrous results. Suddenly Genesis chapters two and three begin to make sense.

And what about the second of our questions above? Why should a loving God give any instructions at all? In many ways the answer to that is simple. It is because he loves us. He made us to be in relationship with him and obedient to him so that we might enjoy his blessings. Just as I am concerned that my children grow up being happy and knowing they are loved, so God's concern in creation was that we know and love him. I would not be a loving father unless I gave my children a framework which, I hope, will be for their good and growth. Of course, I will do that imperfectly, but God never will.

So the instruction God gave was for the good of mankind. But as mankind was tempted by the serpent to rebel against God, those very words of God were twisted. They doubted God's word:

> [The serpent] said to the woman 'did God really say
> "you must not eat from any tree in the garden"'?[21]

The answer to that question is of course 'no'. God did not say
that they could not eat from any tree in the garden. He simply
said that they could not eat from the tree of the knowledge of
good and evil. The words of God had been taken and twisted.
Even the woman's reply betrayed a lack of clarity:

> The woman said to the serpent, 'We may eat fruit
> from the trees in the garden, but God did say, "You
> must not eat fruit from the tree that is in the middle
> of the garden, and you must not touch it, or you will
> die."'[22]

It is much the same in the twenty-first century. Time and time
again I meet people who reject the Bible as God's word to us.
Often I ask them if they have ever read it and frequently the
reply is 'no'. Or some people have read some of it, but misuse
what they find for their own ends. A man might want to leave
his wife. He reads that God is love, and as he is in love with
another woman he decides that he should leave his wife
because that is what the God of love would want – even
though the Bible states explicitly that he should not leave his
wife. So often we doubt God's word, or we simply fail to
understand it. But in doing so, we sanction our own behaviour,
we set ourselves up as the ones who decide what is right and
wrong. We decide what is best, even if God has instructed

otherwise. We mock and doubt his word — often with disastrous results.

MANKIND_DOUBTED_GOD'S_MOTIVE

The dialogue between the woman and the serpent continues:

> 'You will not surely die' the serpent said to the woman.
> 'For God knows that when you eat of it your eyes will
> be opened, and you will be like God, knowing good
> and evil.'[23]

I doubt whether many of us express our decision making in the terms 'I will be like God.' The concept that there is a God is far from the minds of many — the notion of wanting to be like him is even more ridiculous. But in effect it is what we all do. If we are created in the image of God to be in relationship with him, living under his rule (as the Bible says we are), then the only alternative is that we live out of relationship with him, not under his rule but ours.

Morality then becomes what I decide to do. The concern I have is first and foremost for me. Even those I love I do so conditionally — what I get out of a relationship determines what I put in. My money, my job, my aspirations all become centred on me. This is what the Bible calls 'sin.' Others may couch it in different language, but the reality remains the same. It is the concern to be 'No.1':

> Human societies are the most complex of all animal
> societies. There is a continual pressure to be 'No.1'[24]

Being 'No.1' means that I sit 'on my own throne'. I become the boss of my own life, I make the decisions of what is right and wrong, I look out for my own interests . . . . I reside in Genesis chapter three.

MANKIND_DOUBTED_GOD'S GOODNESS

We have already seen that God had mankind's best interests at heart. But somehow the man and the woman doubted the character of God. He had told them that they were free to eat of any tree in the garden, apart from the tree of the knowledge of good and evil. So much to enjoy — and all with their best interests at heart. And yet they rejected it. They gave up so much simply because they doubted God's motives (and his goodness). They were tempted to think that he had said what he did because he wanted to protect himself, that he didn't want them to know too much in case they rebelled!

It is crazy to have such a notion of a good God. He had given them so much to enjoy. After all, they were his people and he wanted them to enjoy his blessing. To think otherwise is to project the thoughts and emotions of sinful man onto God — again something which we do so readily in our own day and age. It takes a different form of course. We view it as the power and oppression of the church, the manipulation and fear generated by Christians to frighten people into commitment. It is so easy for us to distort God's word and so distort his character or to distort his motives and so exonerate our negative response.

But scripture is clear. His motive is love, perfect love and he does have our best interests at heart. If he created us, it should come as no surprise that he longs to be in relationship with us and longs to bless us.

SIN_AFFECTS_US_ALL

The word 'sin' evokes different pictures in our minds. Sometimes we associate it with images on television advertisements – cream cakes we shouldn't eat or even, as with one advertisement, cars we should buy. Perhaps we associate with things we would like to do but might feel a little guilty about – however innocent or otherwise those thoughts might be. Or maybe it is a word which we reserve for those who murder, rape, steal and commit fraud; a word which we certainly wouldn't apply to ourselves.

When we read the Bible we realize that sin is not simply something that 'other people' do. It is a condition which affects us all. We have all set ourselves up in the position of 'boss,' we have all made ourselves the Lord of our lives. Even if we accept some of the teaching, or ideas, or concepts of the Bible, we don't live in relationship with the creator. In short we have all 'sinned'. If you are not sure that you are a 'sinner' then try these two tests:

a) Imagine that you are sitting in a room with your closest friends. In front of you is a large television screen. As you look up you realize that what you are watching is a record of your life – everything you have ever said or thought or done, in public and in private. How would you feel? Yes, there would be many good scenes before us – those times we have been kind and generous and loving. But I expect that if we are honest, all of us would be embarrassed and ashamed by the majority of what we saw – everything we had ever thought, or said or done, publicly or in private. It doesn't bear thinking about!

b) Look at your diary and your bank account. In what way do they demonstrate your concern to live in relationship with God? Would someone be able to recognize you as a person who seeks to love God in everything you do by the way you use your money and your time?

The reality is that we all fall short. We have all sinned. It is just as the Bible says: 'All have sinned and fall short of the glory of God.'[25]

Just imagine for a moment if there was no sin in the world. We would have no need of a police force, armed services, locksmiths, charities, prisons; we would need fewer lawyers; there would be no poverty, no crime, no sadness, no breakdown of relationships; children would know they are loved; marriages would work; there would be no drug abuse or alcohol abuse . . the list is endless. But it is far from reality. The truth is that sin is in the world and I am sinful. We have all rebelled against God, whether we like it or not. This side of Genesis three humanity was and is sinful. That is why the world, created to be so good, is also so bad and so ugly.

MANKIND IN REBELLION

III

WHAT_ABOUT_SUFFERING?

I don't think I would be far off the mark if I said that everyone who might be reading this book has been affected by the pain of suffering — either directly or indirectly. We might have lost a loved one after years of suffering, or a child who died prematurely through illness or a tragic accident. We might watch the television and see the devastation of lives and livelihoods following the earthquake in India or the genocide in Kosovo. We might look back to the events of the last century and to the millions of innocent Jews killed in the Second World War, or the trench warfare and human devastation of the First. It causes us to raise our hands in horror and our fists in anger. And we cry, with some justification, 'if there is a God, why does he allow this?!'

I can't offer easy answers; there is no neat package which tidies up our emotions and makes us smile again. Suffering affects us all and it is painful. For some it raises personal and emotional questions, for others intellectual; for many it raises both. If we have any belief in God we can be left wondering whether God is all powerful and not all good or whether he is all good but not all powerful. Surely if he was all-good and all-powerful he would remove suffering? It seems enough to induce atheism. Our sentiments echo the words of Somerset Maughan:

> I'm glad I don't believe in God. When I look at the misery of the world and its bitterness, I think that no belief can be more ignoble.

But the Bible hits that world of bitterness head on and helps us to find answers in the face of suffering.

In_the_beginning

In one sense God is sovereign over all. He is all-powerful and he could remove suffering if he wanted to do so (we shall return to this later). But we must not think that he created suffering out of vengeance or hatred. In the beginning the world was perfect in every way. God looked at all that he had made and said it was 'very good'. Suffering only began when the created rejected the rightful rule of the creator, when the relationship was severed. God-centredness was exchanged for self-centredness and harmony was exchanged for disharmony. We see the effects of this in the world today.

The constitution of UNESCO at the United Nations states 'Since wars begin in the minds of men it is to the minds of men that the defence of peace must be construed.' In other words, it is because of what we are on the inside that conflict is as it is. Not surprisingly these words echo those of Jesus 'From within, out of men's hearts come evil thoughts, sexual immorality, theft, murder, adultery, greed, malice, deceit, lewdness, envy, slander, arrogance and folly.' The diagnosis made by Jesus and UNESCO is the same, but all attempts at treatment devoid of God have failed. After the war to end all wars we have had a century riddled with conflict.

Even the created order itself has been thrown out of joint. So what was created to be good and perfect also bears the marks of the creature's rebellion. What we see now is natural decay, disintegration and disaster. Creation itself 'suffers' and needs to be restored.

What was good has become marred. The relationship with God has been severed and the consequence of that has affected the rest of the created order. Personal and global relationships are damaged (leading to estrangement and war) and the created order is distorted (leading to natural disaster and difficulty in food and energy production). It all comes from a rejection of the creator.

AT_THE_CROSS

We only have to look at the cross to see the extent of God's love for a suffering world. It shows us that God entered into our suffering and dealt with it. Many of us might wonder how a God 'up there' could know or feel anything about us 'down here'. But we must remember that at the heart of the Christian faith is Jesus Christ, the 'God-man' who 'though he was rich, yet for your sakes he became poor, so that through his poverty you might become rich.'[26] The Word (Jesus) became flesh and dwelt among us and in dwelling among us he experienced more pain and suffering than many of us will ever experience.

The short playlet entitled 'The Long Silence' encapsulates much of the reality of what Jesus experienced.

At the end of time, billions of people were scattered on a great plain before God's throne. Most shrank back from the brilliant light before them. But some groups near the front talked heatedly — not with cringing shame but with belligerence.

'Can God judge us? How can he know about suffering?' snapped a pert young brunette. She ripped open a sleeve to reveal a tattooed number from a Nazi concentration camp. 'We endured terror . . . beatings . . . torture . . . . death!'

In another group a Negro boy lowered his collar. 'What about this?' he demanded, showing an ugly rope burn, 'Lynched . . . for no crime but being black!'

In another crowd, a pregnant schoolgirl with sullen

eyes. 'Why should I suffer' she murmured, 'It wasn't my fault.'

Far out across the plain there were hundreds of such groups. Each had a complaint against God for the evil and suffering he had permitted in his world. How lucky God was to live in heaven where all was sweetness and light, where there was no weeping or fear, no hunger or hatred. What did God know of all that man had been forced to endure in his world? For God leads a pretty sheltered life, they said.

So each of these groups sent forth their leader, chosen because he had suffered the most. A Jew, a Negro, a person from Hiroshima, a horribly deformed arthritic, a thalidomide child. In the centre of the plain they consulted with each other. At last they were ready to present their case. It was rather clever.

Before God could be qualified to be their judge, he must endure what they endured. Their decision was that God should be sentenced to live on earth — as a man!

'Let him be born a Jew. Let the legitimacy of his birth be doubted. Give him a work so difficult that even his family will think him out of his mind when he tries to do it. Let him be betrayed by his closest friends. Let him face false charges, be tried by a prejudiced jury and convicted by a cowardly judge. Let him be tortured. At the last, let him see what it means to be terribly alone. Then let him die. Let him die so that there can be no doubt that he died. Let there be a great host of witnesses to verify it.

As each leader announced his portion of the sentence, loud murmurs of approval went up from the throng of people assembled.

And when the last had finished announcing his sentence, there was a long silence. No-one uttered another word. No-one moved. For all suddenly knew that God had already served his sentence. [27]

God entered our suffering in Jesus Christ, which means that he can totally identify with us as we experience suffering ourselves. It is remarkable when we think about it. Unlike any belief system in the world, God became man – in history, in the person of Jesus. What is more remarkable is that he came into the world simply because he loves us. Humanity had rebelled against God and yet God's love was unstoppable. God came for a rebellious people, a people who wanted nothing to do with him, a people who would rather live their own way than his, a people like you and me. And he came with the sole purpose of dealing with the root cause of that suffering.

Later chapters will explain why Jesus died on the cross. But fundamentally it was in his death that he dealt with the consequence of our rebellion. Our relationship with God had been broken. Jesus came to restore it. And that restoration of relationship which he achieved by dying on the cross was the most costly form of suffering anyone had ever devised:

Crucifixion seems to have been invented by 'barbarians' on the edge of the known world, and taken over from them by both Greeks and Romans. It is probably the most cruel method of execution ever practised, for it deliberately delayed death until maximum torture had been inflicted.[28]

The cross was and is the means by which suffering has been defeated. The cross is all about God restoring us to a pre-rebellious state, a state free from suffering. But the world is not yet free from suffering. One day it will be.

AT_THE_END

We might well see that in the cross Jesus experienced suffering at its worst. And as we read further chapters we might understand how the cross achieved the restoration of relationship between God and man. But we are still left with a world in which suffering is rife. Theories of the cross do not destroy the reality of pain.

The Bible starts with a picture of perfection — the world in its pre-suffering and pre-rebellious state. It also ends with a picture of that creation restored, a new heaven and a new earth in which there will be 'no more death or mourning or crying or pain, for the old order of things has passed away.'[29] That change, or restoration, is brought about by the death of Jesus on the cross. If we trust Jesus Christ (and so come back into relationship with God) that perfection will be ours — we will experience paradise.

It all sounds too neat, doesn't it? I'm writing about an event which happened two thousand years ago, the ultimate benefit of which I will not receive until I die – and only then if I trust Jesus. It seems no more than 'pie in the sky when you die.' That may be so – you must decide. But before you do, think of the alternative.

The alternative is that God wipes out all suffering. After all, if he is the all powerful, all knowing God presented in the Bible, then surely he could do just that. But what would the consequence be? All of us would agree that suffering is 'less than perfect,' incompatible with a perfect God. He could indeed remove it all when he wanted. He could remove all suffering and all who have contributed to suffering in any way – all those who have ever hurt anyone, neglected anyone, acted selfishly towards anyone. The trouble is that he would also have to remove and destroy you and me, for we too live in this world of suffering and contribute to it. We have played our part, even through apathy, of making it what it is, some of us to larger extents than others.

No, what many of us want is for God to destroy what we don't like and don't want in the realm of suffering, whilst turning a blind eye to the suffering we might inflict on others, through our words and actions. But a perfect God will act in a perfect way. He does not want to destroy his creation, he wants it to return to him. That is why he sent Jesus into the world, dealing with the problem and identifying with our suffering in one agonizing execution all those years ago.

A sufferer from skin cancer would know the futility and desperation of treating his skin with cosmetics. It might look better but it would not deal with the real problem. But once the real problem is treated he will know that recovery is in sight. A perfect treatment would ensure a perfect recovery, but he may still experience some of the symptoms until that treatment takes effect.

So it is with the cross. God has done all he needs to do in Christ. The treatment is complete, but we do not yet see the full results of the treatment. The symptoms are still with us. But one day, there will be perfection again, paradise restored – all in Christ and because of Christ. God could remove all suffering now, but if he did he would remove all opportunity for us to return to him. We would be wiped out, destroyed, unable to respond to the real treatment – the forgiveness and restoration that comes in Christ. Surely a loving God wouldn't do that?

IN_THE_MEANTIME

One irony of the times in which we live is that we in the West are surrounded by material comfort. We have warm homes, decent clothes and medication. At the same time we live in one of the bloodiest and most dangerous periods in history. I often wonder whether our cocooned comfort and the discomfort of the world has caused many who call themselves Christians to expect God to give them an easy life, removing all suffering and difficulty. However, the Bible might cause us to think differently.

It is clear from the New Testament that God gives his people love and peace in abundance. But those same people often experienced real suffering. The apostle Paul is a great example. He gave up a comfortable and prosperous life to follow Jesus. As a result he often experienced what many would regard as 'severe suffering.'

> I have been in prison more frequently, been flogged more severely, and have been exposed to death again and again. Five times I received from the Jews the forty lashes minus one. Three times I was beaten with rods, once I was stoned, three times I was shipwrecked. I spent a night and a day in the open sea, I have constantly been on the move. I have been in danger from rivers, in danger from bandits, in danger from my own countrymen, in danger from Gentiles, in danger in the city, in danger in the country, in danger at sea; and in danger from false brothers. I have laboured and toiled and have often gone without sleep; I have known hunger and thirst and have often gone without food; I have been cold and naked.[30]

Paul also had physical ailments which caused him to cry out to God in prayer. We don't know exactly what this ailment of ailments was, but he describes his condition as 'a thorn in the flesh, a messenger from Satan.' Although Paul prayed, God did not alleviate the problem. Instead he said 'My grace is sufficient for you, for my power is made strong in weakness.'[31]

The apostle rejoiced in his sufferings because they taught him about God and taught him dependence on God.

The New Testament goes even further. It warns (or

perhaps encourages?!) Christians that they will suffer by virtue of being Christians. For some that may mean martyrdom – it is estimated that this year about 160 000 Christians will lose their lives because of their faith – but for others it may be no more than ridicule and hardship from non-believers. Whatever the Christian may experience, the Christian will suffer.

But God can use suffering for his glory. Someone who is ill and near death may find themselves asking what life is all about – and may come to faith in Jesus Christ. We must not mock such testimony. I am not surprised that many ask about the real issues of life and death when those very issues are immediate to them. Suddenly material possessions and aspirations fade while relationships and eternity loom large.

We need to look back to creation and mankind's rebellion to understand why suffering is in the world. We need to look back to the cross to understand how God has both entered this world of suffering and dealt with its root cause. And we need to ask the real questions that suffering brings, knowing that God can use it and that one day he will remove it.

3

MANKIND
UNDER
JUDGMENT

MANKIND_UNDER JUDGMENT

I

God will not let our rebellion go on forever. If he did nothing about it, he would not be loving. If he said it did not matter, he would not be just.

The Bible makes it clear that the just and loving God will deal with our rebellion. He will give us what we ask for. In rebelling against him and resisting or rejecting his rightful claim on our lives, we are in effect claiming that we want to live without him; we would rather live our own way, whatever the consequences. And so God will give the rebel what he chooses and what he deserves. If we choose to do without God in this life, we will be without him in the next. The breakdown of relationship will be permanent.

But as God is the source of life and all good things, a permanent estrangement from him will mean being cut off from all that is good and all that is of God. It will mean death and hell.

God's judgment against rebels is an everlasting and God-less death.

The Bible never deals with this subject lightly. It is horrific. But the message of the Bible is how God himself has initiated a rescue plan, intervening in this world so that we could be rescued from hell for heaven.

MANKIND_UNDER JUDGMENT

II

'Forty years ago we stopped believing in hell; twenty years ago we stopped believing in heaven.'[32]

The word 'hell' is off the agenda of most churches. Even though it might be declared formally in church services, it is often rejected personally. But strangely the word has not disappeared from secular culture. Rather it has been redefined. Hell is now used to describe discomfort, irritation, a bad journey; it is used to entertain and make us laugh. So now we have neighbours from hell, or drivers from hell. We have advertisements with angels on clouds wanting their bread toasted 'by the man with the fork downstairs.' We have little devils encouraging us to eat cream cakes and we have pictures of men dressed in red with horns and tails.

It is all a joke, imagery of bygone years which once scared a medieval population and is now used to entertain a modern one. Even if the possibility of the existence of hell does filter back into the consciousness of the average person, it is almost thought to be a good, fun place.

Our imagery and definition of hell has been moulded by a culture of misunderstanding. But the Bible tells me that the consequence of my rebellion is hell. This chapter will look at the whole issue of hell and judgment again – its reality, the reaction to it and the reason for it.

THE_REALITY_OF_HELL

We must say at the outset that to speak of hell at all should fill most people with abhorrence. We have already seen the necessity of a just judgment, indeed we have seen that inbuilt desire in us all for such judgment (usually of others!) And I expect that we can cope with the logic and necessity of God exercising perfect judgment – a judgment which highlights my imperfection all the more, just as a coat of fresh white paint on a dirty wall makes us realize just how 'un-white' the old wall was and how much it needed painting! But hell? Is that the consequence of God's just judgment? The thought of it can fill us with disgust and disbelief. And perhaps it should. C.S. Lewis, in his defence and explanation of this judgment of God, wrote:

> There is no doctrine I would more willingly remove from Christianity than this... The doctrine is intolerable.[33]

But Lewis went on to show that:

> it has the full support of scripture and, specially, the
> Lord's own words. It might surprise us, but as we look
> at the Bible, it is Jesus more than anyone else, who
> spoke of hell. Indeed, much of the graphic language
> about hell comes from the Lord Jesus himself.[34]

It is intended to shock, to make us think. Medieval art may
have told only part of the story, and left us with a picture of
judgment without love, and punishment without mercy. But in
the modern rejection of the image we have often failed to
grasp what those images seek to convey – the reality of an
eternity without God, a godless death. And it is a reality,
explained by the Bible in several different ways.

PUNISHMENT

Jesus said 'Then they will go away to eternal punishment, but
the righteous to eternal life.'[35] It seems a stark contrast and
one which causes many to question the justice of God. But we
must remember that injustice only occurs when the
punishment does not fit the crime.

This was brought home to me in a rather trivial way as I
sat watching a video of *Wind in the Willows* with my children.
Toad of Toad Hall, the notorious scoundrel, is up before the
magistrate for stealing a car and driving too fast. He is
sentenced to twenty years imprisonment in a deep dark
dungeon. Great fun for kids (and their parents) but a totally

disproportionate sentence for poor Toad. We may feel the same about God's judgment. And certainly, if our wrongdoing is not deserving of such a punishment, then God is indeed unjust. But in God's eyes, sin is serious – so serious in fact that it took a divine, selfless initiative to deal with it. We only need to look at the cross to realize what lengths were required to deflect the punishment and pardon us, (of which more later).

DESTRUCTION

Jesus said 'do not be afraid of those who kill the body but cannot kill the soul. Rather, be afraid of the One who can destroy both soul and body in hell.'[36] Again, the language is strong and frightening. Those who first heard these words would have been very aware of Gehenna (the word here translated as 'hell'), a rubbish dump outside Jerusalem that was both obnoxious and offensive. A Jew would have been ritually defiled by association with it. So the language is strong and the picture is clear. Jesus wants his listeners to realize that it is a terrible thing not to be in the presence of the living God. The Biblical alternative to heaven is hell.

EXCLUSION

In telling the story of the rich man and Lazarus, Jesus shows the great gulf between heaven and hell: 'And besides all this, between us and you a great chasm has been fixed, so that those who want to go from here to you cannot, nor can anyone cross over from there to us.'[37] The Bible is clear, heaven and hell are poles apart. After death it is not possible to move from one place to the other. Our rebellion against God puts us on course for hell. On our own we cannot turn round and head for heaven. Only by turning to Jesus can we have any hope. His death took the judgment of God for me.

The language is strong. It is frightening. And yes, I think it is meant to scare. If a child was running to a cliff edge, unaware of the awful possibility of what might happen if he didn't stop, his father may well shout 'Stop'. The language is firm, even frightening, but the motive is love and the result is a child who is saved from a terrible accident. It is the same with God. The words describing hell and judgment may be frightening, but the motive of God is love, and a right response will result in a saved life.

We cannot be absolutely sure of the precise nature of hell 'but clear and definite we must be that hell is an awful eternal reality. It is not dogmatism that is unbecoming in speaking about the fact of hell. It is glibness and frivolity. How can we think about hell without tears?'[38]

God's whole concern is that we might go to heaven. The Bible tells us again and again that he does not delight in the death of a sinner. Rather, the judgment of God which leads to the Godless death that is hell is the result of our own choosing. If we decide to do without God in this life we will be without him in the next. And all that we will experience will be devoid of what we now experience from God in this mixed world of good and bad and ugly. Is friendship good? We will experience none of it in hell. Is God good? We will experience nothing of him in hell.

One Christian minister I know was on his way to speak at a small town in Australia. As he travelled he got talking to a man who said that he wanted to go to hell. 'All my friends will be there,' he said. 'I don't doubt it', replied the minister, 'but you won't know them.' Hell is devoid of any of the good gifts we now enjoy from the giver. We may enjoy some of them now but 'death removes this last contact.'[39] The unbeliever 'has his wish — to live wholly in the self and to make the best of what he finds there. And what he finds there is hell.'[40]

God wants us to be in heaven. But he cannot simply jettison justice so that we might get there. How could *he* say that wrongdoing does not matter? *We* hate being cheated, robbed, lied to, abused, raped. We despise murder and war. How can we expect God to turn a blind eye to such wrongdoing? We need absolute justice. But absolute justice brings absolute consequences.

REACTION_TO_HELL

The doctrine of hell is an uncomfortable one and it can cause us to ask some fundamental questions about the character of God. Broadly speaking, our reaction to hell might be emotional, intellectual or moral.

EMOTIONAL_REACTION

The emotional reaction to hell is an understandable one. Hell is too terrible for words. Those who laugh at hell either do not believe it exists or have redefined it. Hell is a horrible place. But as we react with emotion, let's remember that the whole mission of Jesus and the message of the Bible is one of rescue. God so loved the world that he sent Jesus so that all who believe in him should not perish but have everlasting life.

Hell is a just judgment. When we are wronged we want justice. We want the wrongdoer to be punished. When God was wronged he wanted justice, but instead of punishing the wrongdoer, he took the punishment himself. Perhaps our emotional reaction should not be shock at the reality of hell, but at the reality of God's initiative to rescue us from it.

INTELLECTUAL_REACTION

In early twenty-first century, when many have forgotten God and most have abandoned hell, it is more likely that our reaction to the judgment of God will be one of intellectual doubt rather than emotional trauma. We assign such barbaric notions to the middle ages and before – a cruel and crude doctrine of yesteryear. We say 'It is barbaric. We are civilized.' However, three comments need to be made to those who would hold this objection:

i) Our civilized society may not be as civilized as we think. It is more sophisticated than previous ages and we are more sanitized to the barbarism of life, but the heart of man has not changed. Half the countries belonging to the United Nations still practise torture; there is still war, death and discrimination. Civilization has made us less crude but no less cruel.

ii) The pictures and language used to convey the reality of hell are 'out of date.' For many of us, Gehenna means nothing and darkness can be alleviated by electric light – but we must be careful not to reject the reality simply because we don't identify with the image used to convey it.

iii)   Most importantly, humanity remains the same. If we are to reject hell on intellectual grounds, we must assume that it was only there in the past because humanity had not understood what it now understands; and that with increased knowledge there was a decreased acceptance of and need for hell. But as we have seen, humanity is still in rebellion against God. Greed, selfishness and egotism are timeless – the spiritual realities of life, the need for forgiveness and reconciliation, the certainty of death and the questions it brings remain forever real; as does the historical reality of Jesus Christ.

Intellectual growth has not removed the consequence of sin, it has just given us more opportunities to express it. In which case, hell too remains a reality.

> For those who are perishing, responsible for their unresolved rebellion against God's rule, there is the pain of exclusion from the presence of God in hell, forever; of failure to become what they could have been; of the inconsolable loss of that love that should be at the centre of human life . . . there need be no doubt that this has been their own choice in not wanting to be ruled by God, but we can hardly think about it without pain and horror.[41]

MORAL_REACTION

As we contemplate the horrific consequences of not being in the presence of God in eternity, it is appalling. As a clergyman taking funerals it becomes all too easy to question one's own belief as grieving relatives talk of the love and kindness which typified the life of their recently deceased husband or father or friend. The temptation, (and indeed the hope of many who are bereaved), is to say that all will go to heaven, that all will be right in the end, regardless of belief. It would be so much easier and so much less painful. None of us wants those we love to be somewhere other than heaven — to say or suggest otherwise leads to the moral reaction and revulsion at the prospect of hell.

But as we look at the Bible and the world, we are left with little alternative:

i) If all go to heaven regardless of belief, then what about murderers, rapists, child abusers, Hitler? Should they go to heaven? To say 'yes' we would have to say that justice and punishment do not matter, that criminal and victim can happily exist in eternity with no consequence for either. If we say 'no' then we are drawing a line, making a judgment, by which we are deciding who is in and who is out. But how would we decide? What if someone had not murdered but had committed grievous bodily harm — would they be allowed in? As soon as we fall below the absolute, it becomes very difficult to have any form of 'justice.' Equally, as soon as we speak of absolutes, we all fall short — none of us can go to heaven. We need someone who can get us there. We need Jesus Christ. So we come back again to the gospel message — God has set the standards and we all fall short. But God has provided a way out, if only we would accept him.

ii) The loss of loved ones is painful. It hurts. Death seems an intrusion to life. However much we can rationalize its inevitability or explain it away, it is never easy. It is as if something unwelcome has intruded into a world which was created to be good and just and complete. But that is exactly it. Death has intruded. It is the consequence of sin. A Christless death does cut us off from God, it is painful, it is unwelcome, it is unnatural. That is why God sent Jesus. And in order to remedy the problem *he* had to die.

Moral questions are real, but we must not use them to create an illusion that all will be well. If that were the case, then Jesus would never have needed to come. But he did. His death was a rescue — from hell for heaven.

REASON FOR HELL

Hell is an uncomfortable doctrine. It would be so much easier to say that it does not exist and that all will go to heaven. But a moment's thought will not allow such deception. Heaven must be perfect. Anything short of perfection would result in a heaven full of the pain and injustice of earth. It would be dominated by a God who said that such pain and injustice did not matter, that it was of no consequence. It would not be a better world because any hope of justice would have been buried in the plains of eternity. There would no longer be any way of saying what was right and wrong. If God no longer had any concerns for what was right and just, then we would have no means of appeal. No, for heaven to be heaven, described in the Bible as a place free from the 'old order' of crying and pain and mourning, it must be perfect. And just as a glass of pure water becomes impure with even a single drop of impure water, so heaven would cease to be heaven if even the smallest 'sin' was tolerated.

It means that as we stand you and I are not fit for heaven. We are not perfect. We all fall short of God's standard. We have all 'sinned' and are not fit for God's presence. But the whole desire of God is to rescue us from this world and its sin – and the love of God drove him to do it in the only way which was just and loving.

'Here is a true saying and worthy of full acceptance; Christ Jesus came into the world to save sinners'.[42]

Mankind_under Judgment

III

What_about_those_who_have never_heard?

As people examine the Christian faith sooner or later they come to this question. It is no surprise really when we think about this vast and varied world in which we live. Many people have not heard about Jesus and many of those who have heard have been misled. What happens to them? Are they consigned to hell?

It is an understandable question, but equally, it is a question which can only be asked by those who have heard. And it can only be asked by those who have begun to understand the realities of heaven and hell for themselves. If we think all are saved, then the question would not concern us. If we think all religions are the same – or that it doesn't matter what we believe, it probably would not concern us either. After all, most peoples in the world have some belief system, even if it is only animism. So the fact that the question is asked is a good thing. It shows an understanding of the predicament we are all in and a concern for those who haven't had the opportunity to repent.

But underlying the question there is another more fundamental question about the character of God – namely, is he just? In my experience the people who have asked me this question are those who have had a genuine concern as to whether or not God is fair in his dealings with mankind.

Two responses might help place this question within a Biblical framework;

1. The Bible makes it very clear that all humanity is sinful, that all have rebelled against God, even if they don't know it. The apostle Paul's letter to the Christians in Rome makes it very clear 'There is no-one righteous, not even one; there is no-one who understands, no-one who seeks God. All have turned away, they have together become worthless; there is no-one who does good, not even one.'[43] When we see humanity through the lens of the Bible, all humanity is in the same boat. We have all fallen short of God's standards. If on the other hand mankind is morally neutral, then it would be totally unjust for anyone to suffer the punishment or wrath of God. God would therefore be unfair to those who have never heard of Jesus.

2. The Bible makes it clear that God is completely just. He will deal with all people with complete justice, whether or not they have heard of Jesus Christ. We know that this is true

because we are told in the Bible that God will 'judge the world with justice by the man he has appointed [Jesus Christ].'[44]

If these two points are true (as the Bible says they are) then it means we can have confidence in God as he deals with those who have never heard of him or his plan of rescue. What we cannot do is to speculate on unusual cases. God is just and will deal with all people justly.

But it must be remembered too that God's concern was that humanity should come to know him. The last instruction Jesus gave to his disciples was 'To make disciples of all nations.'[45] In the 2000 years of Christian history, that has certainly happened. The church (followers of Jesus) has grown from a bewildered core of twelve to millions of people and has representatives in almost all countries of the world. As I write and as you read, men and women are putting their trust in Jesus Christ and Christians are sacrificing all to tell those who have not heard.

So we must ask ourselves why it is that we are concerned for those who haven't heard. Is it because we ourselves don't trust the character of God, or is it that we ourselves know the character of God but are finding an excuse not to put our trust in him? The question which perhaps should cause us more concern is 'what about those who have heard?' If we have heard the gospel and we understand what it means, then we will have little excuse when it comes to facing God. He has given us a means of rescue. Will we accept it?

PART_II

WHAT_HAS_GOD DONE?

4

JESUS

JESUS

I

The story thus far has been rather depressing. God as creator will judge his rebellious creation. It is clear what we need saving from.

But Christianity is all about **GOOD NEWS**. The whole Bible is ultimately about God's mission to rescue his people. Because of his love and mercy, God has not left us to the consequences of our rebellion. Instead, he has taken the initiative to save us by sending his own Son into the world.

Jesus was born as a man, grew up in an ordinary family and experienced all the pressures and pain of life, just as we do. But unlike us, he never sinned. He lived as humanity was designed to live, obedient to God, loving his heavenly father and loving those around him. He lived a perfect life.

And yet despite the fact that he had the power to raise a child from the grave, to feed a hungry crowd and to walk on water, he was executed by crucifixion. Even as the crowd jeered and mocked he remained hanging in pain — simply because he knew that was why he had come into the world.

The Bible tells us that Jesus came into this world to save sinners. He came to die as a substitute for you and me. He was innocent; we are guilty. Jesus died in our place, taking the punishment for our wrongdoing on himself. Although we deserve to be where he was, he died in our place so that we might be freely forgiven, able once again to enjoy friendship and fellowship with God.

JESUS

II

Everyone seems to have an opinion about Jesus. We may not know anything about him, but we seem to be able to make a comment — often negative and usually incorrect. If we were asked about some other figure of ancient history we would probably be more honest. But with Jesus we all claim to know.

It is rather strange that we should know anything at all about a man who ended up being executed as a common criminal. He never wrote a book; he never led an army; he never travelled more than 200 miles from his birth place; he had a few followers, most of whom deserted him and denied knowing him when he was arrested. And then he died, executed as a criminal in a provincial outpost of the Roman Empire.

Yet this man changed history — our dating, our culture, our legal system, our educational system and the belief which has dominated vast amounts of the world for the last 2000 years, all stem from this one individual who died as a young man after a short time in the public eye. Contrast him to another man who lived a hundred years later. Ben Kosiba was captured and beheaded by the Romans after a three year war. He had been the leader of a major Jewish uprising in which more than half a million Jews were killed, fifty fortresses destroyed and almost a thousand villages razed. He had land deeds in his self-appointed title of the 'President of Israel' and coins minted as such. Even the leading rabbis of the day hailed him as the Messiah. And yet outside his generation, virtually no-one has ever heard of him.[46]

Jesus Christ, on the other hand, is a name which is known the world over. The documents which record his life and teaching are part of the world's best selling book. In our own day and age he continues to arouse respect and interest. Billy Connolly said of Jesus 'I can't believe in Christianity, but I think Jesus was a wonderful man.' Spike Milligan was once asked whom he would most like to meet. Without hesitation he said 'Jesus.'[47]

Whatever we think of Jesus, it is clear that he has made a real impact on history. And as we turn to the Bible, its pages and its message are dominated by the life and death of this man.

THE_LIFE_OF_JESUS

The Gospels make it very clear that their purpose is to communicate Christ. Mark starts his Gospel like this: 'The beginning of the gospel about Jesus Christ, the Son of God.'

He doesn't leave us in much doubt. The gospel (another word for 'good news') is about Jesus. It is good news about Jesus. That's a shock in itself. Many people either assume Christianity is about church (with old buildings and clergy wearing old clothes) or about being good. For so many the word 'Christian' has been wrenched from its roots. The Christian message is good news. And it is about Jesus Christ.

> The person and work of Christ are the rock upon which the Christian religion is built. If he was not who he said he was and if he did not do what he said he had come to do, the foundation is undermined and the whole superstructure will collapse. Take Christ from Christianity and you disembowel it; there is practically nothing left. Christ is the centre of Christianity; all else is circumference. [48]

JESUS' TEACHING WAS ABOUT HIMSELF

As we go on in the gospel of Mark we get a further shock. Jesus' ministry begins with these words 'The time has come, the Kingdom of God is near. Repent and believe the good news.'[49] It is only when we understand that the good news is about Jesus Christ that the shock becomes apparent. Jesus was saying 'The time has come, repent and believe *in me.*'

I often hear people say that they respect Jesus because he was a good teacher. But I have yet to meet a good teacher who simultaneously says that he himself is the content of his own teaching. However able that teacher was at communicating his chosen subject, I would sincerely doubt his sanity or his sincerity.

But Jesus' teaching focuses entirely on himself. He didn't come to bring a moral code or a set of guidelines that we must follow. He came to show us who he was and what it means to follow him. We must reject the notion that he was simply a good teacher or a moral teacher. C.S. Lewis reminded us of the foolishness of assuming Jesus to be just a great moral teacher:

> I am trying here to prevent anyone saying the really foolish thing that people often say about him: 'I'm ready to accept Jesus as a great moral teacher, but I don't accept his claim to be God.' That is the one thing we must not say. A man who was merely a man and said the sort of things Jesus said would not be a great moral teacher. He would either be a lunatic — on a level with a man who says he is a poached egg — or else he would be the devil of hell. You must make your choice. Either this man was, and is, the Son of God: or else a madman or something worse. You can shut him up as a fool, you can spit at him and kill him as a demon; or you can fall at his feet and call him Lord and God. But let us not come with any patronising nonsense about his being a great moral teacher. He has not left that open to us. He did not intend to.[50]

JESUS'_TEACHING_IDENTIFIED_HIM_AS_GOD

We are so familiar with the picture of the meek and mild do-gooder that is comes as quite a shock to think that many people over the years who have made similar claims have been diagnosed as mentally unstable, even dangerous. In all that Jesus did and said there was no mistake that he was claiming to be God in the flesh.

In the Old Testament, God symbolically dwelt in the temple in Jerusalem. It was the centre of Jewish life and worship. Yet when Jesus arrived on the scene he claimed to replace it. The temple was the point at which man and God met, through sacrifice. In claiming to replace the temple, Jesus was saying that he was now the point of contact between man and God, the place where God would meet his people. It was the most arrogant of claims. He was in effect saying 'if you want to see God, look at me. If you want to come to God come through me.'

We only have to read through the gospels to see quite how outrageous Jesus' claims were. In Mark's gospel Jesus claimed the prerogative of God alone when he forgave the sins of the paralysed man (Mark 2). He could just have made the outrageous claim and pronounced forgiveness, but in order to show that he had both authority and power to forgive sins, he healed the paralysed man in front of the crowd. The irony is that the religious leaders were not so concerned about the miracle as the claim to forgive sins. 'Who can forgive sins but God alone?'[51] they said. The whole point was that only God could forgive sins. And therefore when Jesus made such a claim, he was claiming to be God.

Likewise John's gospel is full of outrageous claims. In one confrontation with the authorities, Jesus said 'before Abraham was born, I am.'[52] He was thereby claiming to be both pre-existent (i.e. he 'always was') and divine. The term 'I am' was the title with which God identified himself to Moses in the burning bush.[53] Jesus wanted others to be very clear that he was God in the flesh. Make no mistake, says Jesus, 'if you have seen me, you have seen the father.'[54]

Even the briefest of readings of the gospels will show us that Jesus' teaching showed him to be God incarnate.

JESUS'_TEACHING_SHOWED_HIM_TO_BE
THE_CENTRE_OF_HISTORY

A new millennium brings with it all sorts of questions about history. There would be nothing to celebrate were it not for the fact that we base our dating on a man whom many regard as irrelevant. And yet the gospels paint a different picture – Jesus is presented as the centre of all history, fulfilling all that had gone before and providing the solution to mankind's rebellion against God. The four gospels begin in different ways, but all are at pains to point out that the one who was about to arrive was the long promised and long expected saviour.

Matthew begins his gospel by showing that Jesus was the 'Son of David, the Son of Abraham.'[55] He thereby identified Jesus as the fulfiller of two great Old Testament promises – that God would establish a king forever on the throne of David[56] and that he would bring a great nation into existence who would rejoice in the blessings of God (the 'offspring' of Abraham).[57] The one who was to fulfil all God's promises was here.

Mark moves straight into the story of John the Baptist – Isaiah promised that God would send a messenger ahead of him to prepare the way of the Lord. And so John came, fulfilling the promise of Isaiah and pointing to Jesus.

Luke begins with information about the birth of Jesus but just before Luke begins his record of Jesus' ministry, he provides us with a detailed genealogy of Jesus' ancestry. At first sight it appears rather odd until we see that the genealogy goes back to Adam. Luke wants to make it very clear that Jesus is descended from Adam. And the reason why that is so important is because of a promise God made way back in Genesis 3. Adam and Eve had just eaten the forbidden fruit and in the middle of the curse which followed, God made an extraordinary promise. He promised that a descendant of Eve would be the one who would undo the work wrought by the serpent (a term used for Satan in the Bible). In other words, remedy for man's rebellion and the destruction of Satan would come about through a descendant of Adam and Eve. And as Jesus begins his ministry, Luke is at pains to tell us all that the long awaited Satan crusher is here.

That is why when we go to traditional carol services it always begins with a reading from Genesis 3. But it ends with a reading from the beginning of John's gospel.

John begins his gospel with these words: 'In the beginning was the word [Jesus] and the word was with God and the word was God . . . . The word became flesh and dwelt among us.' It is a reminder not simply that Jesus existed but that he was God. It is no surprise then that Jesus spoke to people in the way he did. He wanted those around him to know that he wasn't just a prophet or a good teacher, or a miracle worker, but that he was the promised one, the centre of history, the fulfiller of the promises of God. And so as the religious leaders diligently studied the Old Testament, he said to them 'You diligently study the Scriptures because you think that by them you possess eternal life. These are the Scriptures that testify about me, yet you refuse to come to me to have life.'[58]

Jesus knew very clearly who he was and why he had come, even if at first others did not. After his resurrection Jesus appeared to two rather bewildered and confused disciples travelling on the road to Emmaus. As he listened to their story about the events in Jerusalem and the death of the one they had hoped was 'going to redeem Israel,' 'Jesus replied "How foolish you are, and how slow of heart to believe all that the prophets have spoken! Did not the Christ have to suffer these things and then enter his glory?" And beginning with Moses and all the prophets, he explained to them what was said in all the Scriptures concerning himself.'[59] Jesus knew that he was the centre of history and that in him it was possible to be forgiven and restored to God.

THE_CHARACTER_OF_JESUS

It was once said that character is what you are when you are on your own. It is a precious commodity and all the more so when it is open for scrutiny and attack — as Jesus' was and still is. His enemies looked long and hard to find something that would incriminate him, something that would reveal a chink in his armour which could be exploited, but they found nothing. In fact, when persecuted and under great physical strain, Jesus' character came out with even greater clarity and strength. Earlier in his ministry he had preached a sermon in which he said 'Love your enemies and pray for those who persecute you.'[60] And sure enough, as Jesus looked down at his tormentors from the cross, he did just what he had asked others to do 'Father, forgive them, for they do not know what they are doing.'[61] What he said and what he did matched. His enemies couldn't find fault with him.

Neither could his friends. Most of us know ourselves and our friends too well to suppose that they would say we were perfect. If they did make such a claim we either wouldn't believe them or would wonder what it is they wanted. But this is what one of Jesus' closest friends said of him: 'He committed no sin and no deceit was found in his mouth.'[62]

Jesus was perfect. He was loving and kind, he treated all people in the same way — young and old, rich and poor, male and female, Jew and Gentile. And yet he died the most disgusting and well known death in history. It is only as we understand why he died that we will understand the Christian message — and just why it is good news.

The_death_of_Jesus

The Christian faith does not have many symbols. But if there is one symbol known to all of us, it is the cross — the symbol of degrading suffering and shame. Our familiarity with church buildings and jewellery might cause us to be rather numb to the offence of the cross. But imagine for a moment a stranger from another country, free from the familiarity of this particular symbol of execution:

'Walking along Fleet Street, he is impressed by the grandeur of the building's proportions, and marvels that Sir Christopher Wren could have conceived such an edifice after the Great Fire of London in 1666. As his eyes attempt to take it in, he cannot help noticing the huge golden cross which dominates the dome.

He enters the cathedral and stands at its central point, under the dome. Trying to grasp the size and shape of the building, he becomes aware that its ground plan, consisting of nave and transepts, is cruciform. He walks round and observes that each side chapel contains what looks to him like a table, on which, prominently displayed, there stands a cross. He goes downstairs into the crypt to see the tombs of famous men such as Sir Christopher Wren himself, Lord Nelson and the Duke of Wellington: a cross is engraved or embossed on each.

Returning upstairs, he decides to remain for the service which is about to begin. The man beside him is wearing a little cross on his lapel, while the lady on his other side has one on her necklace. His eye now rests on the colourful, stained-glass window. Though he cannot make out the details from where he is sitting, he cannot fail to notice that it contains a cross.

Suddenly the congregation stands up. The choir and clergy enter, preceded by somebody carrying a processional cross. They are singing a hymn. The visitor looks down at the service paper to read its opening words:

> We sing the praise of him who died,
> Of him who died upon the cross;
> The sinner's hope let men deride,
> For this we count the world but loss.

From what follows he comes to realize that he is witnessing a Holy Communion service, and that this focuses upon the death of Jesus. For when the people around him go forward to the communion rail to receive bread and wine, the minister speaks to them of the body and blood of Christ. The service ends with another hymn:

> When I survey the wondrous cross
> On which the Prince of glory died
> My richest gain I count but loss
> And pour contempt on all my pride.
>
> Forbid it, Lord, that I should boast,
> Save in the cross of Christ my God;
> All the vain things that charm me most,
> I sacrifice them to his blood.

Although the congregation now disperses, a family stays behind. They have brought their child for baptism. Joining them at the font, the visitor sees the minister first pour water over the child and then trace the cross on his forehead saying 'I sign you with the cross, the sign of Christ, do not be ashamed to confess the faith of Christ crucified . . .'[63]

The Christian faith is dominated by the cross. What was a symbol of barbaric execution has become a badge of honour – so much so that the apostle Paul could say 'May I never boast except in the cross of our Lord Jesus Christ'[64] and 'For I resolved to know nothing while I was with you except Jesus Christ and him crucified.'[65]

If we read the biographies of famous people, the vast majority of what we read is about their life. The only reason we remember their death is because they had a famous life. Three people die every second, and although it is devastating for the immediate family and friends, the vast majority of us are not affected. We only know about the death of famous people because their life brought fame. But Jesus is different, not only because he became 'famous' by his death rather than his life (even though he died as a friendless common criminal) but also because the accounts we have of him are dominated by that death (unlike all other 'biographies' which are dominated by life). One third of Matthew, Mark and Luke and one half of John's gospel are devoted to the last week of Jesus' life. Clearly it is important. Jesus, an innocent man, dies and his death dominates the New Testament.

Let's look at what Matthew's gospel has to say about his death:

In the same way the chief priests, the teachers of the law and the elders mocked him. 'He saved others' they said 'but he cannot save himself! He's the king of Israel! Let him come down now from the cross, and we will believe in him. He trusts in God. Let God rescue him now if he wants him, for he said "I am the Son of God."' In the same way the robbers who were crucified with him also heaped insults on him.

From the sixth hour until the ninth hour darkness came over all the land. About the ninth hour Jesus cried out in a loud voice, 'Eloi, Eloi, lama sabachthani' —which means 'My God, my God, why have you forsaken me?'

When some of those standing there heard this, they said, 'He's calling Elijah.'

Immediately one of them ran and got a sponge. He filled it with wine vinegar, put it on a stick, and offered it to Jesus to drink. But the rest said, 'Now leave him alone. Let's see if Elijah comes to save him.'

And when Jesus had cried out again in a loud voice, he gave up his spirit.

At that moment the curtain of the temple was torn in two from top to bottom.[66]

Jesus died. He died in agony, executed as a common criminal. But his death was more than the end of an otherwise outstanding life. On the cross, 'God was in Christ reconciling the world to himself.'[67] There, on the cross, outside Jerusalem,

2000 years ago, the most cosmic event in history took place — the means by which human beings could be reconciled to their creator. When Jesus died he both acted as a substitute for us (he took our place) and as a satisfaction for sins (he took our penalty).

SUBSTITUTION

The crowd mocked him, the sky went dark and Jesus cried out some little understood words declaring that God had abandoned him. But this was not the simple death of a would-be messiah. Rather it was the turning point of history. God incarnate was stepping into the shoes of humanity and dying in our place.

THE_MOCKING_DISSENTERS

Jesus died the most disgusting death in history. And as he hung there on the cross, nailed, naked and in pain, those who saw him mocked. Before him and around him were the supposedly righteous of the day (the chief priests, teachers of the law and elders) and the unrighteous (the robbers who were crucified with him). They had seen his miracles and knew that he had the power to save life. But it wasn't his miracles they denied, it was his identity. They could not accept that he was the Messiah, God's king in God's world, especially now that he was hanging on a cross as a despised common criminal. And so they taunt him. If only he would get off the cross and save himself. Then they would believe that he really was the King of Israel – the one he had claimed to be all along.

And yet they unknowingly speak with great irony. They make the same mistake that we make today when we cry out 'if only God would do something to make the world a better place. If only he would do something about the suffering and the pain and the injustice.' The crowd wanted Jesus to get off the cross and save himself in order to demonstrate that he really was God's king in God's world. If we had been there no doubt we would have said the same. But what they had failed to realize is that it was only because Jesus was God's king in God's world that he stayed on the cross – not to save himself but to save others. For there, outside Jerusalem Jesus died, 'the righteous for the unrighteous, to bring you to God.' (1 Peter 3:18)

All along Jesus had known that he was heading to this bloody death outside Jerusalem. By his actions and his words he had made it clear that death awaited him – a death in which he would be a substitute for others; a death in which he would 'give his life as a ransom for many' (Matthew 20:28). Even his name, Jesus, was given 'because he will save his people from their sins' (Matthew 1:21). On the cross he was doing just that. And he was the only one qualified to do it. Only because he was the King of Israel, the Son of God, was he able to take our place – and therefore our punishment – on the cross. No one else had the qualifications to do it because no one else was sinless.

If we discovered that we were all in financial debt, then only someone who had an infinite amount of money could hope to help us. Even if my debt was great and yours was small, you would not have the means to help me. It is just the same with our sin. I may be the world's most corrupt person, my sin might be very 'public' and you might be relatively 'righteous' in the world's eyes. But neither of us can help ourselves or each other. We have all sinned. We need someone who is infinitely righteous, infinitely sinless to help us. And there has been only one who has met such high credentials — Jesus, the Son of God, the king of Israel. Only Jesus was qualified to pay for our sins. And that is exactly what he did on the cross outside Jerusalem. He stayed on the cross to save others because he was God's king in God's world. He was the only one who could be our substitute.

THE_MIDDAY_DARKNESS

As Jesus hung dying on the cross, darkness covered the land. For three hours in the middle of the day, it was dark. Some have tried to explain away the darkness as a natural phenomenon such as a solar eclipse, but it just won't fit. For those of us who have experienced a solar eclipse we will know that it does not last three hours. I was standing in the car park of Legoland in Windsor in the summer of 1999 when the eclipse occurred. The temperature fell and the light became a dusty silver, but it soon passed. An eclipse just would not last three hours. It will not explain what happened at Calvary. Neither will any of the alternative physical solutions which have been put forward. But that is perhaps because the explanation is not physical but spiritual – not geographical but theological.

We need to look to the Old Testament to understand why it went dark in the middle of the day. Eight centuries before Jesus came the prophet Amos spoke God's word to God's wayward people. His message was a message of judgment and one of the pictures and promises of judgment involved midday darkness:

> In that day, declares the Sovereign Lord, 'I will make the sun go down at noon and darken the earth in broad daylight'.[68]

When the darkness appeared at the crucifixion it was the judgment of God. But on what – or whom? In the Old Testament judgment always fell on those who were rebellious against God – those who had not lived as God's people in God's world; those who had taken the good gifts but ignored the giver. People just like you and me. No doubt they did good things and enjoyed good things – as we do, but they failed to live as God wanted them to live. Even those who were religious used their religion as a mask for their greed, corruption and wickedness. Like us they had no difficulty in dressing up for religious occasions. Like us they knew what to say and what to do. They would have had no trouble in using the 'church' for weddings and baptisms and funerals. But when it came to their hearts, that inner secret world which spills out more than we would like – that world of thoughts and actions that we wouldn't always want others to see – they were rotten to the core and deserving of the judgment that Amos promised.

But Jesus was different. No one could find fault with him. He had lived in perfect relationship with God. His heart was pure. Yet at Calvary, on the cross, he faced the judgment of God – a judgment that he did not deserve; a judgment which was and is rightfully ours. On the cross he was our substitute.

THE_MEANINGFUL_DECLARATION

Just before Jesus died he cried out in anguish, 'My God, my God, why have you forsaken me?' Throughout the gospels Jesus had expressed intimacy with God . . 'All things have been committed to me by my Father. No-one knows the Son except the Father, and no-one knows the Father except the Son and those to whom the Son chooses to reveal him.'[69] Jesus had called God 'Father' and revealed the Father to men and women. Yet here on the cross that same God abandoned him. Here is God's king in God's world, the perfect sinless man. Why should God abandon him when the Bible makes it clear that it is only the sinful who are spiritually abandoned and cut off from God?

The answer lies in the fact that Jesus was in just that situation. Though sinless himself he had gone to the cross to pay for the sin of others. Although he was God's king in God's world he had come to die for the world which rebelled against him – a world of which you and I are a part. That world mocked him, as it still does. It still wants him to get off the cross and do something to show that he is the king. But Jesus stayed on the cross as the king, abandoned by his Father as he shouldered the judgment that we deserved. His death instead of mine.

The story is told of a group of POWs during World War II who were working on the Burma Railway. At the end of each day's work the tools were collected and counted. One day a guard became furious because he thought that a shovel was missing, so much so that he threatened to kill all the prisoners if it was not returned. At that moment a man stepped forward and said he had lost it. He was clubbed to death, paying for the crime of the missing shovel. The prisoners then returned to the camp only to discover than the shovels had been miscounted. The one man had sacrificed himself for the others. His death had been a substitute for theirs.

And in a similar way, Jesus' death was a substitute for ours. The difference – we are guilty, deserving of death – and the one who pronounced the sentence was the one who paid the sentence. Nothing we do makes us worthy to be right before God, nothing we attempt is acceptable to him. However hard we might try, our acts of goodness will not deal with the problem of our hearts. We may try and try but we will fail – we continue to be riddled with pride and selfishness.

A couple of years ago I had to go to hospital to be treated for acute renal failure. For the eight days before I was admitted the problem was not diagnosed. No one knew what was wrong with me. Although I was given all sorts of pills, none of them sorted out the problem. There was nothing wrong with the pills in and of themselves. They just couldn't treat my condition. It is the same with all the 'good' things we do. Nothing is wrong with them in and of themselves, but they will not treat our condition. And just as I needed dialysis, a more radical treatment, so we need a more radical spiritual treatment to put us right with God. The cross is that radical treatment. Only there can we be put right with God. Jesus died in our place. He died as our substitute.

SATISFACTION

I have never been to see a Grand Prix. Living where I do means I often hear cars racing, but I have never been to a race. I suspect that if I were to go most of the team tactics would be beyond me. I wouldn't know which cars were adopting a two or three pit-stop race or why. But if I was watching the race on television, I would have a much better idea of what was going on. The commentator would explain who is stopping when and why. The commentary would explain the action.

It is the same in Matthew's account of the cross. He supplies a commentary to help us understand what was going on when Jesus died on the cross. We are taken back to the Temple, inside the city walls of Jerusalem, and to the central chamber, the Holy of Holies. This was the place where God symbolically dwelt and where only one man, the High Priest, could go only once a year. Even then he could not enter until he had undergone an elaborate ceremony. After an animal had been sacrificed for the forgiveness of his own sins (its death instead of his), he then went into the Holy of Holies to perform the same action on behalf of the people. God was so holy that no one could stand before him — their sin was too great.

Jesus died. And the curtain which separated the Holy of Holies from the people tore — from top to bottom. It could not have been done by human hands, the curtain was too large and inaccessible. It must have come from God. Suddenly the way to God was open. No more sacrifices were needed. It was possible to come into the presence of God without a priest and the ritual that went with him. Why? Because at that moment, outside the city walls, a once-for-all, final sacrifice was being made. Jesus was that sacrifice. He so dealt with the problem of sin that no further sacrifices were needed. His sacrifice was sufficient satisfaction for our sins.

It is an amazing gift. God says that either we can pay for our sins — with a godless death; or we can accept Jesus' payment for us. It is a simple choice, but one that we have to make. 'For God so loved the world that he gave his one and only Son that whoever believes in him shall not perish but have eternal life.'[70]

JESUS
III

CAN_WE_TRUST_THE_BIBLE?

Throughout this book I have quoted fairly freely from the Bible. And perhaps you are wondering if that is really fair. After all, the New Testament was written by Christians, so it is inevitably going to explain the Christian message and the Old Testament seems outdated and made redundant by the New Testament. Is it therefore reasonable to use it as 'proof' of the Christian faith? Is it trustworthy? Can I really believe what it says?

This section will attempt to answer those questions by looking at the external evidence relating to Jesus, the trustworthiness of the documents themselves and the internal claims of the Bible.

EVIDENCE_RELATING_TO_JESUS

It would be foolhardy to say there is much evidence relating directly to Jesus from non-Christian sources. But that does not mean for a moment that he did not exist or that there is no objective history in the New Testament accounts. It must be remembered that Christianity started after Jesus died and, more importantly, after he rose from the dead. Before those events Jesus was in many ways no more than one of the many political figures of the first century.

The New Testament emerged from the politically traumatic world of the first century. And in that world many of the disciples and others misunderstood the nature of Jesus' messianic mission. To Jews in an occupied country, as Judea was, they could have no greater hope than for a warrior king who would restore the fortunes of the people of God to their Old Testament ideals. But as we read through the gospels and epistles it becomes clear that although Jesus was seen as a fulfiller of Old Testament hope, his mission was frequently misunderstood. When the disciples identified Jesus as the Christ, Peter then proceeded to rebuke him when he began to teach that he must suffer, be rejected, die, and rise from the dead. Clearly before the resurrection the disciples had little idea as to what Jesus had actually come to do.

So it is no surprise that during his life, Jesus was seen as no more than a radical, a nuisance to the authorities. As such they would have had no need to produce any more documentation on him than they would have had to on any other first century troublemaker. And such records — of anybody – seem not to survive. It is therefore no wonder that the majority of evidence relating to Jesus is Christian evidence. As Christianity did not start until after Jesus died, any non-Christian evidence is likely to be in the form of discussions relating to this new and problematic movement rather than about the person of Christ himself as we have in the gospel accounts.

Coupled with that it should be remembered that Galilee and Judea were two minor administrative areas in the Roman Province of Syria and the Jews, the race into which Jesus was born, were a 'strange remote people little understood and little liked.'[71]

That said, there is a certain amount of evidence which relates to Jesus and to Christianity, a brief selection of which is outlined below.

TACITUS

Tacitus was a gentile writer active during the second century. He is the first Roman historian to mention Christ. In his 'Annals' (c.AD115) he describes the great fire of Rome during the reign of Emperor Nero and the subsequent persecution of Christians:

> To dispel rumour, Nero substituted as culprits and treated with the most extreme punishments some people, popularly called Christians, whose disgraceful activities were notorious. The originator of that name, Christus, had been executed when Tiberius was

emperor by the order of Pontius Pilate. But the deadly cult, though checked for a time, was now breaking out again not only in Judea, the birthplace of this evil, but even throughout Rome.[72]

Although some have questioned how Tacitus might have come across this information, it does show that Jesus was spoken of and written about outside an immediate Christian tradition.

SUETONIUS

Suetonius was a Roman writer who lived from AD69 to AD140. He wrote of Christians as a 'class of men given to a new and wicked superstition.' In his 'Lives of Caesar' (AD120) he mentioned both the persecution of Christians under Emperor Nero and the expulsion of Jews from Rome. 'He expelled the Jews from Rome because they were rioting at the instigation of Chrestus.'[73]

While some have questioned how useful an external reference to Christ this is, Suetonius does mention the expulsion of Jews from Rome, which is clearly attested in Scripture. 'Claudius had ordered all the Jews to leave Rome.' (Acts 18:2)

PLINY_THE_YOUNGER

Pliny was governor of Bithynia from AD111-113. He wrote many letters to Trajan about the administration of the province, which seemed to be suffering from a growth in Christianity. He said that 'many of all ages and every rank' were involved and that like a spreading disease 'not only the cities, but also the villages and the country' were affected. He also described the Christian custom of holding weekly meetings to sing praises to 'Christ as god.'

Clearly by the time Pliny wrote, Christianity was well established and Christians were known for worshipping Jesus as Lord.

JOSEPHUS

Josephus was a Jewish writer who was born in AD37. He wrote two major works: *The Jewish War* and *Jewish Antiquities*. It is the second of these which is important for our purposes, in which Jesus is mentioned twice in the six books devoted to the reign of Herod the Great. Perhaps the most controversial of these two is the *Testimonium Flavium*,[74] a statement which was preserved by Christians, but which may have been amended for their purposes:

At that time there appeared Jesus, a wise man, if indeed someone should call him a man. For he was a doer of startling deeds, a teacher of people who receive truth with pleasure. And he gained a following both among many Jews and many of Greek origin. He was the Messiah. And when Pilate, because an accusation made by the leading men among us, condemned him to the cross, those who had loved him previously did not cease to do so. For he appeared to them on the third day, living again, just as the divine prophets had spoken of these and countless other wondrous things about him. And up until this very day the tribe of Christians, named after him, has not died out.

Although most would agree that this has been amended by Christians, there is enough substance to authenticate the existence both of Jesus and those who followed him.

The second reference is less controversial. In it we are told that Ananus, the newly appointed High Priest, 'convened a court of the Sanhedrin and brought before them the brother of Jesus the so-called messiah, and some other men, whom he accused of having broken the law and handed them over to be stoned.'[75]

We might be surprised at the small number of references relating to Jesus, but for the Jew, Jesus was a rebel and a lawbreaker and once executed was insignificant. He held no place in Jewish history for those who failed to understand him and accept him. It is perhaps all the more surprising that Josephus should mention him at all.

What we can say as we look at Josephus and others is that Jesus wasn't simply fictitious. Clearly he existed and following his death there was a movement which grew and developed so much so that within a few hundred years the Romans who had previously persecuted Christ and his church adopted the Christian faith themselves. And here we are, 2000 years later, many miles away from where these events took place, discussing what could have happened. Whatever we make of it, Christianity has had a profound effect on the world.

The existence of the cross itself is a powerful reminder that the barbaric death of Jesus was central to the events of the first century. So inhumane was the cross that the Romans banned it in AD315. Even before that they had regarded the cross as a horror, reserved only for the lowest of the low – the murderers, robbers and rebels – and then only if they were slaves, foreigners or other non-persons. Such utter disgust, coupled with the Jewish conviction that the messiah could never hang on a cross, led many Jews to reject Jesus as their promised saviour. Others regarded the worshipping of a crucified man as no more than 'donkey worship'. And yet the cross remained the symbol at the heart of the Christian faith .... 'It means that the centrality of the cross originated in the mind of Jesus himself. It was out of loyalty to him that his followers clung so doggedly to this sign.'[76] Why persist with such a disgusting symbol of hope, unappealing to so many, unless the event that occurred on the cross and the man who died there were both true and central to the Christian faith?

THE TRUSTWORTHINESS OF THE BIBLICAL EVIDENCE

Although we cannot 'prove' Christianity from non-Christian sources, there is no doubt that Christ was a figure of history. We have seen as much. But as soon as a 'non-Christian' reports on the Lordship of Christ and his atoning death, it will by virtue of its contents become 'Christian'. It is therefore simply not possible to prove all from documents outside the Bible.

But that does not mean we should abandon the Bible. Rather we should ask whether it is trustworthy and reliable.

Unlike so many 'religious books' the Bible did not emerge in a historical or geographical vacuum. Archaeological, geographical and historical evidence are part and parcel of the New Testament evidence. As ancient documents go, the Bible demonstrates a high degree of internal consistency. We would be very hard pushed to place them in the camp of fiction:

> Unless there is good reason for believing otherwise one will assume that a given detail in the work of a particular historian is factual. This method places the burden of proof squarely on the person who would doubt the reliability of a given proof text. The alternative is to presume the text unreliable unless convincing evidence can be brought forward in support of it. While many critical scholars of the gospels adopt this latter method, it is wholly unjustifiable by the normal canons of historiography. Scholars who would consistently implement such a method when studying other ancient historical writing would find the corroborative data so insufficient that the vast majority of accepted history would have to be jettisoned.[77]

Blomberg's thorough analysis of the New Testament and arguments against its authenticity are well worth reading. He provides a scholarly survey of past and present arguments which have attempted to undermine the New Testament documents and so redefine the New Testament Christ. He concludes:

> Although the difficulty in trying to summarize so much detail in short compass has become obvious, an attempt has been made to look at all the main reasons why parts of the gospels have been viewed as legendary or unhistorical. Those reasons all seem unconvincing. The gospels may therefore be trusted as historically reliable.[78]

THE INTERNAL CLAIMS OF THE BIBLE

We began this section by asking whether or not we can accept the Bible for what it is. But it would be wrong to finish without looking at why we use the Bible. For many the Bible falls into one of two camps — either a magic talisman that is to be kissed, revered or dipped into like a crystal ball — or an irrelevant book of antiquity.

Both responses fail to do justice to the world's best selling book.

In the first place the Bible sees itself as inspired by God. But if by inspired we mean that every word in the Bible is literally true, then we would have to say that the Bible is not inspired. It is quite clear that as we read the Bible it uses different literary genres, each of which must be interpreted according to its own literary rules: history as history, poetry as poetry, parable as parable, etc. The psalms talk of rivers that clap their hands and mountains that sing. Those things are not literally true, but that does not invalidate them.

If I was to watch a television play followed by a documentary, I would be able to distinguish which was which. The play might tell me something, it might make a point about life which is true and valid. The documentary would be factual. I can learn from both, but both are different. I interpret them by their own rules. I don't assume the play is a documentary or the documentary a play. So with the Bible. There are different literary genres in operation, each of which must be interpreted according to its own rules. We could not therefore say that the resurrection was fictional – the Bible emphasizes that it is true and that it must be true for the whole of the Christian faith to stand. Equally we don't expect the rivers to clap their hands.

Secondly, inspiration does not mean verbal dictation. Muslims believe that the Koran was dictated to Muhammad by Allah word for word. Christians do not believe that about the Bible. Scripture is clearly portrayed as both the words of men and the word of God. It wasn't plucked out of the sky but rooted in reality, in history and in the experience of everyday people. It is therefore possible to find corroborative evidence to say 'yes, that happened.'

If we are to understand how the Bible is inspired, then we need to look at the Bible itself and to see what claims it makes, both for the Old Testament and for the New.

THE_OLD_TESTAMENT

If you were given a book of several hundred pages and read only small sections of it at any one time and read it very rarely, it would be difficult to follow the story or work out what was going on. Yet so often when we approach the Bible we are in exactly that situation. The Old Testament in particular can be difficult to understand. But as we have seen already, Jesus clarifies it for us.

Luke records for us the appearance of Jesus on the road to Emmaus after his resurrection. Two disciples are travelling along the road, talking about the events of the past few days. Jesus then joins them but they 'were kept from recognising him.' With downcast faces the two disciples tell Jesus about the events of the past few days in Jerusalem . . . 'Jesus of Nazareth was a prophet, powerful in word and deed before God and all the people. The chief priests and our rulers handed him over to be sentenced to death, and they crucified him; but we had hoped that he was the one who was going to redeem Israel. And what is more, it is the third day since all this took place. In addition, some of our women amazed us. They went to the tomb early this morning but didn't find his body. They came and told us that they had seen a vision of angels, who said he was alive. Then some of our companions went to the tomb and found it just as the women had said, but him they did not see.'[79]

The reply Jesus gave is fundamental to our understanding of the Old Testament. He said 'how foolish you are, and how slow of heart to believe all the prophets have spoken. Did not the Christ have to suffer these things and then enter his glory? And beginning with Moses and all the prophets, he explained what was said in all the Scriptures concerning himself.'[80]

It must have been amazing to have heard that sermon. Here was Jesus explaining how the Old Testament pointed to him. Time and time again the point is made, both from the lips of Jesus and those whose intention it was to explain him. Here was not an eccentric first century political leader or religious maniac, but rather the long awaited and long promised saviour. The history of Israel and the collected writings of a nation over hundreds of years were pointing to him.

And it was not only Jesus and the gospel writers who made such bold and seemingly arrogant claims. The apostle Paul, in writing about the Old Testament said that the Holy Scriptures make us 'wise for salvation through faith in Christ Jesus'.[81] The New Testament Canon had not been fixed at the time he wrote — which means that the scriptures of which he was speaking were the Old Testament. In other words, the purpose of the scriptures before Jesus was to make people wise for the salvation which he came to bring.

THE_NEW_TESTAMENT

Augustine, writing many years ago, said 'The New Testament is in the Old concealed and the Old is in the New revealed.' In other words, there is a link between Old and New Testaments. That link is Jesus. If the Old Testament expects Jesus, the

New Testament explains him.

What we have in the New Testament is a collection of documents written by those who were specifically commissioned with the responsibility of proclaiming the teaching about Christ. These apostles were under instruction from Jesus to 'teach others what I have commanded you.'[82] Their message would be his and through that message people like you and me, in the generations who followed, would hear the gospel of Jesus. And he not only provided for us, but we are told he prayed for us – for those who would 'believe through their message.' It is therefore as we read their message in the pages of the New Testament that we hear the words of Jesus.

He said that he would remind his close followers of all things – they would become the ones who would convey the authoritative teaching of Jesus to others; and it is this teaching that we now have in the New Testament.

The 'odd man out' in the eyes of many is the apostle Paul. Far from being a disciple of Jesus, he was a persecutor of Christians. But Jesus called him to be an apostle. Yes, he was different to the other apostles in some ways. He didn't share their 'qualifications' of having known Jesus in the flesh or having seen him resurrected before he went to heaven. But Paul himself realized this all too acutely when he called himself 'the least of all the apostles.' He knew that his qualifications were not the same – but he was still accepted as an apostle by those who were in that close band of disciples. Indeed, Peter referred to the teachings of Paul as 'scripture' long before the New Testament was sorted and bound. In other words his credibility and credentials were accepted and known. What he said was not mere opinion, it was and is the authoritative word of God. In every way he wrote as one of Jesus' commissioned apostles. He was able to instruct the young Timothy with these apostolic words 'what you heard from me keep as the pattern of sound teaching with faith and love in Christ Jesus . . . and the things you heard me say in the presence of many witnesses entrust to reliable men who will also be qualified to teach others.'[83] He introduced himself in his letters as 'Paul, an apostle of Christ Jesus by the will of God.'[84] His words, along with those of others from that apostolic band of witnesses, make up what we have in the New Testament.

The gospels (Matthew, Mark, Luke and John) were written later than the letters of Paul and the other apostles. The church was being persecuted and the first generation of Christians (those apostles commissioned with the truth of Jesus) were dying out. There was a great need to write down concise documents which would explain who Jesus was and why he had come. People needed to know; the generations afterwards needed to hear and Christians needed to be encouraged. So the gospels were written – concise, highly structured theological documents so that people could hear about Jesus and respond to him.

So when we read the Bible and when we talk about it, it is not to be treated as some magical or mystical religious tome. It was written in ordinary language to ordinary people in order that they might know Christ and be equipped to live for him. It is the same today.

5

THE
RESURRECTION
AND_THE
CHURCH

THE
RESURRECTION
AND_THE
CHURCH

I

If Jesus had remained in the grave, death would have had the final say. But death had no hold on Jesus. On the third morning after his death he rose from the grave and was seen alive by hundreds of people.

As a result of the resurrection, it is possible to live the Christian life. It gives the Christian four certainties:

It gives us the certainty that Jesus has

paid the full price for our sins. The penalty of sin is death. Resurrection shows that the penalty has been paid.

It gives us the certainty that Jesus is alive today, as the risen ruler, reigning at God's right hand.

It gives us the certainty that Jesus will come again to judge the world.

It gives us the certainty of the Holy Spirit, the Spirit of Jesus whom he promised for those who believe. Jesus may be in heaven, but as we wait to join him, the Christian has his Spirit. Through that Spirit we can enjoy a relationship with him now and the guarantee of an eternity with him in heaven. As we wait, that same Spirit equips us as his people, the church, to serve him and to serve one another.

THE
RESURRECTION
AND_THE
CHURCH

II

My memory of Easter as a child is somewhat hazy. Chocolate eggs and cards with daffodils occupy the memories I do have and with it the confusion as to how we celebrated the birth of Jesus at Christmas and then, only a few months later, we remembered his death and resurrection. In my childish confusion its significance and centrality completely passed me by.

I suspect that many of us have a similar kind of reaction even as adults. If we don't go to church the Easter weekend is likely to be dominated by gardening, DIY or sport. And if we do go to church we may not fare much better. Those church buildings which are adorned with religious imagery leave us with statues of Jesus on a cross or in the arms of his mother. Rarely do we see him as the victorious and resurrected king. A token model Easter Garden may be left by the main door, only to be taken down once the bank holiday weekend is over. We are left thinking that the resurrection is no more than a postscript to the death of Jesus.

But the New Testament would have us think differently. The apostle Paul wrote 'If Christ has not been raised, your faith is futile.'[85] In fact, 'the entire New Testament was written from the perspective of the resurrection. Indeed, the resurrection may be called the major premise of the early Christian faith.'[86]

So the resurrection is no postscript to the events of the Easter week. It is a foundation to faith, without which we would have no assurance of salvation from sin or the hope of heaven. We would have no certainty about the reality or the rule of Christ. And we would have nothing of the new relationships which typify the church. This chapter will look at the reality of the resurrection, the result of the resurrection and resurrection relationships – and why it is foundational to what we now are – the church.

THE_REALITY_OF_THE_RESURRECTION

I woke up on Easter morning 2000 to a discussion on the radio about the reality of the resurrection. Two of the three interviewed reduced the resurrection to virtual nothingness, assuming that we know so much more in our supposedly sophisticated modern world than that of the first century

Bible writers. In many ways I should not have been surprised. From the early days of the church, people have sought to undermine the reality of the resurrection. But it cannot be dismissed so easily. A number of 'evidential factors' all point to its reality. So much so that Lord Darling, a former Chief Justice of England, said 'In its favour as a living truth, there exists such overwhelming evidence, positive and negative, factual and circumstantial, that no intelligent jury in the world could fail to bring a verdict that the resurrection is true.' So what is this evidence?

THE_EMPTY_TOMB

As we read the gospels, it is clear that the disciples did not really understand what was going to happen to Jesus. After Peter had identified Jesus as the 'The Christ,' Jesus then went on to explain why he had come. 'He then began to teach them that the Son of Man must suffer many things and be rejected by the elders, the chief priests and the teachers of the law, and that he must be killed and after three days rise again.'[87] At this Peter took Jesus aside and began to rebuke him. He couldn't accept that Jesus was going to die – or rise from the dead. The empty tomb was not in the mind of the disciples.

And yet that same Peter addressed a large crowd in Jerusalem a short while later. As he preached his sermon he said that Jesus 'was not abandoned to the grave, nor did his body see decay.'[88] Before the death of Jesus, Peter and the other disciples did not expect an empty tomb. Although Jesus had clearly told them what was going to happen, they did not understand until that first Easter morning when they saw it for themselves. Thereafter there was no doubt in their minds that the tomb was empty.

Of course, the story could have been made up. But if we are to place it in the realm of fiction, we need to overcome a few difficulties. First, the tomb was new[89] and guarded,[90] thus making confusion over the location of the tomb or body difficult, and fabrication of the story almost impossible. Many could have refuted the claim of an empty tomb. Second, women were the first witnesses on the scene. As their evidence was inadmissible in court, a fabricated story would have surely been designed to maximize the likelihood of belief and would therefore have placed men as the first witnesses of the empty tomb.

It is very difficult to come up with any plausible alternative to the empty tomb. Indeed, 'The resurrection kerygma [teaching] could not have been maintained in Jerusalem for a single day, a single hour if the emptiness of the tomb had not been established as fact for all concerned.'[91]

THE_TRANSFORMATION_OF_THE_DISCIPLES

When Jesus died his followers were lost and confused. He was the one for whom they had given up everything, and now he was dead. He had been mocked and humiliated. In Jewish minds he had experienced the curse of God by being hung on a 'tree'. And he had been apparently powerless to rescue himself when during his ministry he had rescued others. The disciples were left leaderless, hiding behind locked doors for fear of the Jewish authorities.

And yet something happened which radically changed these followers of Jesus. When Jesus was arrested, Peter had denied that he even knew him. A few weeks later he addressed a crowded Jerusalem. 'God has made this Jesus, whom you crucified, both Lord and Christ.'[92] There was no longer any need to fear men because Jesus had risen. He had shown himself to be the Lord, the rightful ruler of God's world. There was no longer any need to fear death because Jesus had overcome death. It was the certainty of the resurrection of Jesus which transformed these men, together with the presence of his Holy Spirit, given to the disciples after Jesus rose. And if Jesus is the risen ruler and in his resurrection he conquered the enemy of death then the fear of what man can do becomes insignificant. Indeed the disciples needed to proclaim the resurrection of Christ in order that others would know that Jesus is the risen king before whom they must submit.

Whatever we are to make of the truth of the resurrection, however much our modern minds get tangled up in the scientific difficulties of how resurrection can occur, no one can deny that something happened. The existence of the church today is testimony to the change in the disciples. As the first disciples spoke the message and others came to put their trust in Jesus, so those new converts in turn told others, who told others .... who told us. And so people today still testify to the same transforming power of the risen Lord Jesus.

THE_LACK_OF_A_REASONABLE_ALTERNATIVE

Inevitably many have sought to 'explain away' the resurrection of Jesus. Typically such 'alternatives' fall into four categories.

i) Jesus did not really die. The heat and loss of blood caused him to pass out. He was assumed dead and was taken to the tomb, whereupon he revived in the cool air and 'appeared' again. In their shock, relief and excitement the disciples thought Jesus had risen from the dead.

The difficulties with this theory are numerous. Scourging in those days was often sufficient to cause death in and of itself. On top of that, Jesus had been on a cross for hours in the heat of the day. No pulse, heartbeat or breath is detected. He is assumed dead and is taken to the tomb. His friends depart and a stone is moved across its entrance. Then somehow he revives, removes the stone, fools the guards and returns to his friends. But what then? Why is there no record of continued teaching or miracles? And how did such a great and influential man really die if the cross was not the end? It doesn't fit.

ii) The body was stolen. This is a far more likely scenario if the resurrection didn't happen. The tomb could have been empty and accepted as such simply because the body was stolen. As to the culprits, two options lie before us. First, the authorities could have taken the body. But if that is the case, then why did they not simply present it as proof that the resurrection didn't happen? If they did have the body it would have been very easy to scotch any resurrection rumour as it began circulating around Jerusalem. The second option is that the disciples took the body. At first sight, this looks like a plausible explanation. But we have to remember that although Jesus did tell them about the resurrection before he died, the disciples didn't understand it. And in the gospel records as we have them, they didn't at first believe that the tomb was empty. If they had taken the body they must have somehow overcome their misunderstandings, overcome their fear and been sufficiently confident of the lie to face those very people of whom they were afraid and declare that the crucified Jesus had now shown himself to be Lord and Christ by rising from the dead.

In addition, we have to accept that no-one who knew the truth ever spilt the beans, even though they faced isolation, persecution, imprisonment and death for their story. It is of course possible, but when added to the host of surrounding 'evidence,' the likelihood becomes increasingly remote.

iii) The story was exaggerated. On this theory, something could have happened, but in its telling, the story has been elaborated. But if this is so, how do we determine what is fact and what is fiction? The resurrection appearances meant that many claimed to see the risen Lord. The very nature of resurrection makes it difficult to elaborate – either Jesus did rise or he didn't. The Bible reports the resurrection as historical with spiritual consequences, not spiritual with historical consequences. According to the New Testament, if Jesus did not rise from the dead, then our faith is futile.

iv) The disciples were hallucinating. The difficulty with this is that the Bible states that different people saw Jesus at different times and in different places. On one occasion he was seen by five hundred people at the same time. Such diverse groups of people will rarely experience the same form of hallucination. And although individuals can experience hallucination, they usually take the form of seeing things one wants to see. But there is no evidence that the disciples were expecting or looking for these experiences.

Our twenty-first century scientific minds can sometimes find it difficult to accept the historical truth of the bodily resurrection of Christ. But the alternative is often harder to believe. One man who sought to explore the veracity of the resurrection was all too aware of the academic pressure which had caused him to doubt the truth of the resurrection. He decided to investigate for himself. In describing his quest, he wrote:

> When I first began to study the life of Christ, I did so with a very definite feeling that, if I may so put it, history rested upon very insecure foundations. If you will carry your mind back in imagination to the late nineties [1890s] you will find in the prevailing intellectual attitude of that period the key to much of my thought . . .the work of the higher critics . . had succeeded in spreading a very prevalent impression among young students that the particular form in which the narrative of his life and death had come down to us was unreliable. It seemed to me that if I

could come at the truth why this man died a cruel death at the hands of the Roman power, how he himself regarded the matter, and especially how he behaved under the test, I should be very near to the solution of the problem. I wanted to take this last phase in Jesus' life – to strip it of its overgrowth of primitive beliefs and dogmatic suppositions, and to see this supremely great person as he really was... I will only say that it effected a revolution in my thought. Things emerged from that old world story which I had previously thought impossible.[93]

Frank Morrison, who wrote those words, came to realize that the resurrection was true. For the first time he was able to say with the words of the creed with confidence . . 'On the third day he rose from the dead.'

As we look at the possibilities we may still have questions, but there is enough to say that the resurrection was a reality and its implications, ever real.

RESULTS_OF_THE_RESURRECTION

I suppose a cynic might ask if there are any results of the resurrection. It is true that there is now a world wide community of believers all of whom ultimately owe their existence in earthly terms to those early witnesses who began the process of sharing the faith which eventually came to our ears, but in other ways we look at the world and see no change. There are still wars, there is still injustice and poverty. People still die from disease and natural disasters, many still suffer.

We will not understand the world today unless we understand the world-view of the Bible. Yes, there are still wars, injustice and poverty. Yes, people still die from disease and natural disasters. The world is still full of suffering. But the results of the resurrection mean that one day that will all end. A victory has been achieved which brings with it certain justice and freedom and perfection. A victory over death. A resurrection victory. That victory gives us three certainties.

JESUS_HAS_PAID_FOR_OUR_SIN

I have only been to prison once. It wasn't as a criminal but as a guest of the prison chaplain. As I left to make my journey home that day I was very aware that I was going home – but for those I had left behind, the prison was their home. The day that they walked out through those prison gates would be a momentous day. A day of freedom. A day when they could walk down the street, free from condemnation with their sentence paid. Their very presence outside those prison walls would be testimony to the fact that their sentence had been paid.

In the same way that those prisoners were paying for the consequence of their crime, the Bible makes it very clear that sin has a consequence. That consequence is death. 'The wages of sin is death.'[94] If left to pay it on our own it would be impossible. We could never walk out of the other side; we could never leave the prison. Death would be final.

That is the state we are in without Jesus. We are left

paying for our own sin — a debt which we could never remove. But Jesus died in our place. He paid our debt. And we would only know if that debt had been paid if he came out the other side, if he walked through the prison gates. On that first Easter morning, Jesus did just that. He had paid the price for our sin on the cross. He had died for us. And once the sentence had been paid he came through death to a resurrected life.

My children are quite small — small enough to need help to cross the road. As we stand on the kerb and look left and right, it is not unusual to feel a small hand gently slip into mine. I hold tightly and seek to give the security and certainty which will allow the children to cross. They could not do it on their own. But because I have done it before, because I have crossed roads, they know that with me they will be able to do it too.

And if we are to cross over from death to life, to go through the grave and come out the other side, we need to do the same. We need to slip our hand into that of Jesus. Without him our sin would sentence us to death, a godless eternity. But if we trust the one who has been through death, we can be sure of life beyond the grave. Jesus takes our sin. He pays the penalty for us. Therefore only in him can we get through death unscathed.

It is just as the popular chorus says 'The price is paid, come let us enter in, to all that Jesus died to make our own.'

JESUS_IS_LORD

Many of us are brought up with standard formula for our

prayers and many of those prayers end with the words 'In the name of Jesus Christ, Our Lord.' It seems so easy to say that Jesus is Lord, and yet if we understand what we are saying, we are making a bold statement about who Jesus is and how he relates to the world in which we live.

As the apostle Paul was nearing the end of his life he wrote a letter to a younger minister from his prison cell. In it he summed up the gospel, the good news of Jesus Christ. He wrote, 'Remember Jesus Christ, raised from the dead, descended from David.'[95] As we have read this book we might be surprised by the language Paul used. There is no mention of sin, or the cross. The good news of Jesus Christ is simply related to his ancestry and his resurrection – and yet together they sum up the gospel. They tell us that Jesus is both reigning king and ruling Lord.

I) JESUS_IS_THE_REIGNING_KING

As a child, Christmas always brought with it a sense of excitement. It was mostly related to presents and Santa Claus, but I still remember the feeling evoked by the words of the Christmas story. . . 'today in the town of David, a saviour has been born to you. He is Christ the Lord.' At that stage I had no idea what the words meant, but 'Bethlehem' and 'David' seemed to play an important role – so important in fact that Matthew begins his gospel with a genealogy which traces Jesus back to David, the Israelite king. He wants his readers to understand that Jesus is a descendent of King David.

A study of the family tree of the queen would remind us of her ancestry. It would tell us about the kings and the queens before her — how long they lived and how long they reigned. We don't need a degree in history to realize that when a monarch dies his or her reign ends and the crown passes to the next generation.

But with the ancestry and kingship of Jesus there is a profound difference. Back in the Old Testament, a promise was made by God to King David. God promised that he would establish the throne of the kingdom of David forever. 'Your house and your kingdom shall endure for ever.'[96] The promised kingship was to be an everlasting one. So people began to look for that everlasting king, descended from David, whose rule and kingdom would be established by God.

Then Jesus came onto the scene. Not only is he introduced to us as a descendant of David, but he behaves in distinctly 'kingly' ways. He rides into Jerusalem on a donkey, fulfilling a prophecy about how the king would ride into the city. He speaks of the kingdom of God, a kingdom of which he is the king. And as a king he claims both the right to rule and the right for others to submit to him as king.

The constant Davidic associations make it clear that Jesus is both a promised king and a reigning king. The resurrection confirms that kingship. Jesus has conquered the grave, death has no hold on him. And as a living king he has no need to hand the crown onto another. He continues to live and so he continues to reign. And if he continues to reign, then the right response must be to submit to him as Lord.

ii) JESUS_IS_THE_RULING_LORD

The word 'Lord' is very closely tied to the word 'king'. Jesus has risen from the grave. He therefore continues to reign as king. But the resurrection and his subsequent ascension into heaven demonstrate the nature of that Lordship. When on earth he was despised, ridiculed and rejected. He died the death of a common criminal. When he rose, he rose a victorious king and ascended to the right hand of the Father in heaven, so that now 'God has placed all things under his feet and appointed him to be head over everything.'[97]

If Jesus is the risen Lord, with everything under his feet, we are bound to ask the question — do we live as his loyal subjects or do we remain rebels against him? The cross assures us that our rebellion, which the Bible calls sin, can be dealt with. The resurrection assures us that we can once again return to the fold and come under the rightful rule of the heavenly Lord. It is that relationship which was broken by mankind's rebellion in Genesis 3. It is that relationship which Christ has restored.

JESUS_IS_JUDGE

If we were to describe the world before and after the events of that first Easter, we would probably not see any difference. The pre-resurrection world and the post-resurrection world was and still is marked by the mix of the good, the bad and the ugly. There is still beauty and kindness and love. And there still is ugliness and hatred and injustice. So in what sense has the world changed by the resurrection of Jesus?

In one sense, the world has not changed at all. But in another way there has been a dramatic change which can give us an absolute assurance that all that we see is not all that there is and all that is bad will not last forever. Jesus has risen from the grave. He does reign as Lord. But the Bible tells me he will also come back as judge.

> For he has set a day when he will judge the world with justice by the man he has appointed. He has given proof of this to all men by raising him from the dead.[98]

Our reaction to this is likely to be mixed. If we have understood the Christian gospel, the message of judgment will no doubt bring with it the realisation that many of those we know and love who have not responded to the gospel will be subject to that judgment and the eternal consequences of their rebellion against God. But at the same time it will bring with it an answer to the mess and the muddle we see in the world today. If God had wiped out all sin and evil and suffering when Jesus first came, then he would have wiped out you and me. There would be no chance for repentance, no opportunity of heaven and no hope of an existence with God, free from crying and mourning and pain. So Jesus came to deal with the root cause. And he will come again to take with him those who are his. He will bring a just judgment, where all wrong-doing and evil is finally dealt with and finally defeated. While we wait for that ultimate judgment, there will still be pain, injustice and suffering. But as we wait, there is the possibility of turning to Christ, with the glorious certainty of heaven beyond.

It was in the centre of Athens, as the apostle Paul addressed a religious but ignorant people that he told them of the God who had in the past overlooked such ignorance — but now 'he commands all people to repent. For he has set a day when he will judge the world with justice by the man he has appointed' — that is, Jesus. In his resurrection he gives the guarantee of future judgment and therefore command of present repentance.

RESURRECTION_RELATIONSHIPS

We still have a black and white television set in our house. It is hidden away upstairs and still used every now and then to watch the late news. Unfortunately it doesn't have the two controls which I tend to associate with older television sets — the vertical hold and horizontal hold. As a child it used to amuse me to move the controls and watch the distortion of the picture before me. Equally it was always rather frustrating when those same controls wouldn't adequately clear up a picture which was distorted.

We take it for granted now that our television sets work well. Very few modern sets have the need or means of changing the horizontal and vertical hold. Our television pictures are clear.

When it comes to God, most people do not share that same sense of clarity or certainty. Their relationship with God — the vertical hold, if you like — is not producing a clear picture. God seems unknown, unclear and irrelevant. When it comes to relationships with other people — the horizontal hold, there is often a similar tension. Whilst many relationships are good and bring with them delight and happiness, others are riddled with tension. So often the very reality of love which people seek is extremely difficult to maintain in practice.

The resurrection of Jesus enables a new set of relationships to be formed which clarify both the vertical hold – our relationship with God, and the horizontal hold – our relationship with one another.

A new relationship with God

As Jesus prepared to go to the cross he explained to his disciples what would happen after he had left them. His words are recorded for us in the gospel of John:

> And I will ask the Father, and he will give you another Counsellor to be with you forever – the Spirit of truth. . . . you know him, because he lives with you and will be in you.[99]

Jesus had just told his disciples that he was going to go to the Father. And now he tells them that when he has gone, they will be given *another* counsellor. As far as they were aware, the only counsellor they knew, the only one they had with them, was Jesus himself. But that was exactly his point. Jesus was going to die. He was going to rise from the dead and ascend to the Father. And after that he would still be with them – not physically, but spiritually. That's why he was able to say of the Spirit who was yet to come 'you know him because he lives with you *and will be in you.*' The very spirit of Jesus himself was promised to his disciples.

Two thousand years later we are in exactly the same situation. Jesus is not with us physically. But we can still know him, and we can experience him by that same Spirit given to the first believers after Jesus rose from the dead. And as we know him, so the real figure of history becomes a real figure of today. Christians do not simply look back to the teaching of a great man, or model themselves on someone who was no more than a figure of history. No, Christians look to a risen, living Lord whom they can know by his Spirit.

I want you to imagine that you are visiting London. You have heard that Buckingham Palace is open to the public and you decide to head there for the day. As you approach the gates you notice a man sitting on the pavement. He is poorly dressed and unshaven. In front of him is a tin with a few pence sitting at the bottom and around his neck is a tatty old piece of cardboard with the words 'hungry and homeless' written on it. You feel desperate and as you wonder what to do, you notice that a Palace official is approaching the man to ask him to move – or so you think. But as you listen to the conversation you can hardly believe your ears. The man has been asked to dine with the queen.

Later, in the evening paper, the story makes headline news: 'Pauper to inherit palace.' You read it in a state of shock – not only was the man asked to dine with the queen, but he was told that all he could see was to be his. He was to be adopted into the royal family and treated as a son.

It is a ridiculous story. But the New Testament tells me that God has done just that for those who have turned to Christ. 'For you did not receive a spirit that makes you a slave again to fear, but you received a Spirit of sonship. And by him we cry "Abba, Father". The Spirit himself teaches us that we are God's children. Now if we are children, then we are heirs – heirs of God and co-heirs with Christ.'[100]

Jesus promised that he would give the disciples *his spirit* – a Spirit of sonship, of intimate and perfect relationship with God the Father. It means that those who respond to Jesus are adopted as children of God, with all the rights of sons. We are like the pauper outside the palace. We deserve nothing from God. Our sin has cut us off – but in the death of Jesus our punishment is taken and God's wrath is diverted and as a result of his resurrection, a new relationship is possible in which those who believe become children of God by the presence of his Spirit. 'How great is the love the Father has lavished on us that we should be called children of God.'[101]

A_NEW_RELATIONSHIP_WITH_ONE_ANOTHER

'Love' is a word which has many meanings and is used in a variety of ways. We talk of 'loving' food, or sport or a good joke. We also use it to describe deep and sacrificial relationships as well as shallow self-centred ones. Inevitably then, when Jesus commanded his followers to love one another, we can easily attach a whole range of emotions and ideas to what he meant. But if we want to see real love in action, we need only to look to the cross. There Jesus died for those who deserted him and those who mocked him. He died for the unlovable and the loveless. He died even for those, like the centurion, who officiated at his execution.

Jesus gave a model of what real loving looks like. And the kind of love he demonstrated is the kind of love which should be the mark of those who follow him. The Christian has the Spirit of Jesus within — a Spirit who enables the believer to love in a way that would not otherwise be possible. Just as Jesus loved those who were not lovable, so the Christian is to demonstrate that same kind of love. That love is a mark of true discipleship . . .'A new command I give you: love one another. As I have loved you, so you must love one another. By this all men will know that you are my disciples, if you love one another.'[102]

Many groups in society express a form of love or camaraderie, united because of a class or culture, but the picture of the church in the New Testament is one which transcends such barriers. It is a community which is marked by a qualitatively different love — one which is modelled on Jesus, which is cross shaped and cross centred. A love which is self sacrificial.

In AD125 a non Christian wrote about what he saw in Christians: 'they walk in all humility and kindness, and falsehood is not found among them. They love one another. He that has distributes liberally to him that does not have. If they see a stranger they bring him under their own roof and rejoice over him as if he were their own brother. For they call themselves brothers, not after the flesh but after the spirit.'[103] That is Christian love.

A_LIVING_BODY

The picture of the church in the New Testament is that of one body with many parts. Each part is essential and each part is different, but together they make up a living, functioning unit. A hand cannot function without an arm and an arm cannot function without a torso. As Christians we are dependent on one another in that same way and so to each Christian God has given gifts and abilities for the sole purpose of serving one another and together bringing glory to Christ. These gifts in the New Testament range from administration to teaching – and all function for the greater good of the church.

So the Christian is not alone. And whilst someone doesn't have to go to church to be a Christian, every true Christian is part of a church – a group of believers who love one another and who are equipped with gifts to serve one another. A group of people without love, without those gifts which serve one another and without a thoroughly Christ-centred faith is not a church, even if they meet in the most ornate of buildings.

A_RESURRECTED_BODY

Millions of people play the National Lottery each week. I can't say it is something I would want to do. The vast majority of those will experience nothing but disappointment and perhaps the financial demand of buying yet another ticket. But for the very few their ticket guarantees them a fortune and financial security. As they sit there holding the ticket with the winning numbers on the television screen in front of them, their financial future is secure, even if at that moment they have not received their prize.

In the same way a Christian can be sure of his future. His certainty does not lie in his achievements but in the finished work of Christ on the cross. As I look back to the cross I can be certain of a glorious future in heaven with God – in his presence in the place of perfection. But I am not there yet. The presence of his Spirit gives me a deposit, but the best is yet to come. And I can be sure of that because Jesus rose from the dead. He has dealt with my sin and conquered death. He has also risen to heaven.

The Bible tells me that when Jesus died, I died – to my sin and all that stopped me having a relationship with God. But it also tells me that when Jesus rose, I rose – not physically, but spiritually. There is a sense in which I am now with Christ in heaven. And one day I will be with him in a far more real way, with the physicality that Jesus had when he rose from the grave.

The church is made up of those who have been raised with Christ. And that resurrection gives a whole new set of goals and ambitions, and a whole new perspective on this world and with it the expectations that we might have. We need have no fear of death. We need not be weighed down by the burdens of achievement and success in this life – for we have everything in the next. And we can make it our goal to please the God in whose life our real life is hidden. As we realize the great consequences of the resurrection, we become free to be the people we were designed to be – which is seen this side of heaven in the church.

THE
RESURRECTION
AND_THE
CHURCH
III

THE_CHURCH_IS_FULL_OF_HYPOCRITES

When we think of church, many of us will naturally think either of a denomination such as the Church of England or old buildings, neither of which are features of the New Testament church. For many that image has been a cause for hilarity or despair. The Church of England seems out of touch, out of date and irrelevant. The television presents its clergy as rather well meaning and ineffectual, wandering around picturesque villages drinking cups of tea and judging flower competitions. When we read of 'the church' in the newspapers we see very little other than news of its decline or sleaze among its members. It can be so far from real church and yet it is so often all that people experience.

Even if people are not put off by the public image they can be put off by what they perceive to be the personal image – an image of those who profess to be Christians saying one thing and doing quite the opposite. A survey of over 600 people between the ages of 18 and 30 asked the question 'What is the biggest obstacle which prevents you from believing in Christianity?' A variety of obstacles were put forward, one of which was the church – its image, its teaching or its hypocrisy. Many felt that it was out of date and therefore irrelevant. Others thought that those who were part of the church were not very attractive examples of Christian living. One person said 'I became disillusioned with Christianity after many years of church attendance. I did not see many Christians (including the clergy) who actually followed the word of Christ.'[104]

But whether it is the media image or the comments of others about those who call themselves Christian, we need to ask ourselves a number of questions if we are to overcome the difficulty of hypocrisy – whether real or imagined.

Experience_or_excuse?

The number of people who attend church is said to have declined from 39 per cent of the population in 1851 to 10 per cent of the population in 1989.[105] More recent surveys highlight further decline. It means that fewer and fewer people actually know real Christian people. Whilst those who do have such contacts may have had bad experiences, it is still easier to hold the Christian faith at arm's length by finding a reason to do so. And what better than to hold on to the idea that Christians are simply 'hypocrites', believing a message which cannot be true and trusting in a God who has no power to make any difference.

In saying that we must not belittle those who have had bad experiences. I have had such experiences myself. But how many of us know people who are not merely church goers, or who call themselves Christians simply because they were born in Britain or were baptized as a child, but rather who can say that they trust Jesus as their Lord and Saviour and can testify to his transforming power? It is those people who constitute the true church and no others and only when we see hypocrisy in them can we legitimately make the claim that the church is full of hypocrites.

CHRIST_OR_CHRISTIAN?

You might have read the above and still think the church is full of hypocrites. It is possible that you have suffered hurt or been treated badly by someone who has talked to you about the Lordship of Jesus Christ. What then?

Well, it must be said that no such action is excusable. If a Christian person treats someone with hatred or contempt or arrogance, it is not unreasonable to question why. But at the same time it must be remembered that the gospel, the good news about Jesus, is not for the good but for those who sin. A

Christian person is someone who has discovered Christ and who knows that they are sinful and in need of forgiveness. Trusting Christ brings with it a new life, and a new identity as a child of God. It also brings with it a new power, by his Spirit, to enable the Christian to live a new life. But the new convert is not suddenly removed to heaven. He or she still lives in this world of decay, with a body and a nature that will decay too. And until the believer reaches heaven, he will experience both the joy of the new nature and the pressure of the old. In short, he will make mistakes; he will fail.

And when he fails he needs to come back to the foot of the cross and to say sorry. And just as he receives forgiveness from God through Jesus, so he needs to ask forgiveness from the one he has hurt – for that in itself is a mark of a changed life. Christians will make mistakes – but the mark of a Christian is the recognition of the constant need of Christ. He promises to forgive and he promises to change people by the power of his Spirit.

It has been said that sharing the Christian faith is like one beggar telling another beggar where to find bread. We are all in the same boat needing forgiveness and restoration – even the mistakes of Christians can point others to Jesus, the 'bread of life,' as in making mistakes they publicly show their need for his forgiveness.

There is a popular song with the lyrics 'Sorry seems to be the hardest word.' If it is not on the lips of Christians who make mistakes, perhaps they haven't really realized what Christianity is all about.

CONDONED_OR_CONDEMNED?

True hypocrisy is ugly. It is the wearing of a mask – the saying of one thing and the doing of another. And Jesus hated it. Ironically he saved his most severe criticism for the religious leaders of the day who elevated themselves with the 'holier than thou' attitude which is so unattractive and so off-putting.

It is a real shame if Christians ever give the impression that they are better than others. A true Christian can only be a Christian because they have realized that in and of themselves they have nothing to offer. Their sin has crippled them spiritually and cut them off from God. No matter how smartly they dress on a Sunday morning or how much they seek to do for others – without Christ they are spiritually dead. Anyone who has understood the message of the cross will be humbled because the cross tells me that I cannot do it on my own. It took the death of God's own son to reconcile me to him. And if I cannot do it on my own, then what reason do I have to place myself above others?

Not only that, but the Christian recognizes that others are in the same boat, not better or worse but equally cut off, equally dead – needing that same act of grace. And because it all comes from God's loving initiative, there can be no reason to boast.

And as if to highlight the horror of hypocrisy, the Christian has only one true model of Christian living this side of heaven – that of Jesus Christ:

Who, being in the very nature God,
Did not consider equality with God
Something to be grasped,
But made himself nothing,
Taking the very nature of a servant,
Being made in human likeness.
And being found in appearance as a man,
He humbled himself
And became obedient to death – even death on a
cross.[106]

Hypocrisy is ugly and when those who profess to be Christian engage in it, it seems all the more ugly. But let's remember that Jesus condemned it, died for it and modelled something very different. And at the end of the day Christianity is first and foremost about him.

6

A_New_Heaven and_a_New Earth

A_New_Heaven and_a_New Earth

I

The Bible begins with a picture of perfection. God is in perfect relationship with his people, who are in perfect relationship with one another and the world.

It also ends with a picture of perfection. Heaven is a place which is free from death and mourning and crying and pain – a place where those who have trusted Jesus are free to enjoy his company and sing his praises for ever; a place where people can live as they were designed to live — in an eternal and perfect relationship with God.

In heaven Christians will receive the fullness of what Jesus died to bring them — freedom from sin and adoption into the family of God. No words or pictures are adequate to describe its perfection and beauty. Only when we are there will we realize just how much this world has been corrupted by sin.

A_New_Heaven and_a_New Earth

11

Heaven gets a bad press. It's not that people don't talk about heaven, it's just that the language they use distorts it or destroys it, leaving us with humorous pictures or confused ideas, most of which are far from the picture presented in the Bible.

Many people seem to have one of three ideas about heaven. The first is that it doesn't exist. John Lennon left us those memorable words which have only served to fuel the popular notion that there is no heaven. 'Imagine there's no heaven. It's easy if you try. No hell below us, above us only sky.' It seems very appealing, and in many ways very logical. We can't see heaven. No one we know has been there and come back and all that science tells us leads us to think that it can't possibly exist.

The second idea rather contradicts the first — namely, that heaven not only exists but it exists for everyone, that it is the next stop after death and therefore the place where all loved ones will go, later to be reunited with those they have left behind. Very few families request entirely secular funerals for their loved ones who have died. Most people hope for something more — indeed, I would suggest that most people believe there is something more. And who can blame them? Death is a horrible business. It destroys relationships. It intrudes into life. And however much we may be able to rationalize its inevitability, it hurts. Death is the greatest enemy we face. It is inevitable that those who have lost loved ones hope for more.

The third popular idea about heaven is that it is boring. We only have to watch the television or read magazines to realize that the popular image of heaven is a place with harps, angels and fluffy clouds, but little else. It is portrayed as wet, weak and rather dull — a place where few would want to spend eternity. It becomes the place enshrined by the pop song lyrics 'heaven is a place where nothing ever happens.'

But as we look to the Bible, all three of those false images of heaven are shattered. The Bible tells us that heaven is a place of perfection, where we find a people with their God. It is, for every Christian, a real promise ahead.

A_PLACE_OF_PERFECTION

It is sometimes difficult to find the words to describe our emotions. We might come back from the holiday of a lifetime, so enthusiastic that the words we use are simply inadequate to describe what we would like to say. It is more wonderful than words.

In a similar way, the Bible tells us that heaven is more wonderful than words. It is in every way a place of perfection, which eye cannot see and mind cannot conceive. No emotion or experience we have this side of heaven will prepare us for its perfection and wonder. Even when we look at a breathtaking view we are looking at a world which was created perfect but has been marred by sin. Even when we experience the genuine love and fellowship of other Christians, we are experiencing new life still mixed with the old. Such good things are only a taste of what we will experience fully in heaven. In heaven the old order will have disappeared. 'There will be no more death or mourning or crying or pain, for the old order of things has passed away.'[107] Words therefore will fail us — for no experience we have had will be like it. The nearest description we have is that of Genesis and Revelation.

In Genesis we see perfection. God was in perfect relationship with his creation and his creation was in perfect harmony with itself. God looked at all that he had made and it was 'very good.'[108] But thereafter that which was perfect became polluted by sin. As mankind rebelled against God so the relationship with God broke down. And as his relationship with God broke down, so did all other relationships. Creation became marred and twisted. Mankind was expelled from the garden and its perfection.

But in Revelation we see that perfection restored. Once more God will be among his people and they will serve him.

There will be a new heaven and a new earth, a new place for God to dwell with his people, in which 'Nothing impure will ever enter it, nor will anyone who does what is shameful or deceitful.'[109]

It will be a wonderful place, a perfect place. But as such, not everyone will be there. The Bible has made it very clear that we have all fallen short of the glory of God – we have all sinned. None of us has the right to go to heaven. It is only through the death of Jesus that we can be there – declared righteous not on the basis of our merit but because of his death. Being good is not good enough. However hard I try I will never be fit for this place of perfection. God is simply too holy and heaven too perfect. It is as if I were trying to swim across the Atlantic. I may be a very bad swimmer and only be able to swim a few yards, or I may be a wonderful swimmer and be able to swim miles. But either way, I will not be able to cross the Atlantic. And so it is with heaven. Even those of us who think we are fairly good are not good enough for heaven. When we compare ourselves with those round us all might appear well, but when we compare ourselves with God's standards, we see nothing but sin. We are far from perfect.

Only Jesus can get me to heaven. And therefore if anyone dies without trusting him, they die in their imperfection and sin. Heaven is not open to them.

A_PEOPLE_WITH_THEIR_GOD

The Bible tells us that heaven will be a place where God's people are finally reunited to him – not just spiritually but in the resurrected life demonstrated by Jesus. Those who have experienced new life in Christ this side of the grave will see that new life brought to completion on the other side of the grave – the perishable will be raised imperishable and the mortal will be clothed in immortality. And because there is perfection and God's church is world wide, the community of those in heaven will not be divided by class or culture. Those in heaven come from 'every tribe and people and nation.'[110] There will be none of the animosity and hatred which typifies the relationships we see this side of heaven. There will be no Kosovo or Northern Ireland. Heaven will be full of Christ's people, perfected in him and praising the one who rescued them.

Such is the picture we have in the book of Revelation. There we see the curtain of heaven pulled back to give us a glimpse of what will come. And as we look at this multitude of people from all classes and cultures, we see them surrounding a throne and praising the 'Lion of the tribe of Judah, the root of David'[111] who has triumphed.

But as we look at that throne in Revelation, expecting to see the risen Lord in his glory, the picture we are given is of a lamb 'looking as if it had been slain.'[112] No one could have read that in the first century without being aware of the lambs that were sacrificed – both at the Passover festival where the people remembered how they were released from slavery into freedom hundreds of years before, and as a sacrifice for forgiveness – the lamb dying in their place. And there, on the throne in heaven, we see the Lion of Judah, King

Jesus himself, looking like a lamb — a lamb who died so that we could be free and a lamb who died in our place.

So heaven is where the Christian is heading. It is a place of perfection where all that we see in Genesis is restored. God's people are once again in God's presence. The enemy of death has been destroyed. They are now free to worship the one who rescued them in the perfection of relationship with him and with one another.

A_PROMISE_AHEAD

It is difficult for us to imagine what heaven is like. The Christian experience this side of heaven is mixed. There are great blessings, but there are battles too. Jesus promised both and the early Christians experienced both. And there is no reason to suggest from the Bible that our experience will be any different. A Christian has the reality of the Spirit living within him, making him more like Jesus, enabling him to function with other Christians as part of the church and giving him joy and contentment in the face of difficulty and suffering. But the Spirit is only a downpayment, a deposit which 'guarantees our inheritance until the redemption of those who are God's possession.'[113] There is far more to come.

A few months ago I was camping in the Scottish Highlands with a friend. Although it was summer we camped high with wind and rain forcing us to use rocks to keep the tent secure. As we climbed into our sleeping bags, fully clothed to minimalize heat loss, my friend said dryly 'now I know why people build houses.' It was a long, cold night and it made the return to family and home comforts all the more wonderful.

The contrast between that experience on the mountain and the delights of home is the kind of contrast the apostle Paul wrote about as he looked forward to heaven.

'Now we know that if the earthly tent we live in is destroyed, we have a building from God, an eternal house in heaven, not built by human hands. Meanwhile we groan, longing to be clothed with our heavenly dwelling, because when we are clothed we will not be found naked. For while we are in this tent, we groan and are burdened, because we do not wish to be unclothed but to be clothed with our heavenly dwelling, so that what is mortal may be swallowed up by life.'[114] We so often think of home and life as all that we experience before death. But here Paul says that our true home and real life are what happen after death.

Time and time again the New Testament exhorts its readers to have the right perspective on this life. If our focus ceases to be heaven our expectation and experience will cease to be thoroughly Christian. We will become confused when we suffer persecution or hardship; we will seek the blessings of the next life in this one. We will mistake the tent for the house and be rather dissatisfied with our lot.

The Christian life can only be lived rightly when, through the work of the Spirit, we realize that heaven is not now but ahead. Now we live in a world full of suffering and sickness and sin. Then we will live in perfection. In the meantime we are still in this fallen world, graciously given the Spirit to enable us to live the Christian life while we wait. But if we lose sight of where we are going, there soon becomes little reason to keep going.

In 1952 a long distance swimmer called Florence Chadwick set out to swim from Catalina Island to mainland California. She swam for fifteen hours in the fog that dogged her attempt that day. Again and again she begged to be taken out of the water. Finally, utterly exhausted she just stopped swimming and had to be pulled out of the water by her trainer. Although she couldn't see the coast, it was discovered that she was only half a mile away. In the news conference that followed she admitted that had she seen the shore she probably could have made it. And as if to prove it, two months later, on a sunny day, she did.[115]

If we cannot see where we are going in the Christian life, we are likely to give up. But the gospel brings with it the certainty of heaven. Jesus' death and resurrection assure us of a great future – more than that, he assures us of a guaranteed future.

I recently heard the story of a preacher who had been talking to a group of children in Scotland. He had been looking at Psalm 23 and using it to show how the Christian faith can become real and personal. As the children said the first five words of the Psalm they were encouraged to point to each one of the fingers on their left hand – the – Lord – is – my – shepherd. The preacher then told them how a personal faith in Jesus Christ could make those words real – that it is possible to know the shepherd personally. Those who decided to follow Jesus would then be able to point to each finger in turn, but when they came to the word 'my' they could grasp their ring finger with confidence and say " the -Lord - is - MY - shepherd."

After the talk the preacher returned home, but a little while later he was phoned with some devastating news. One of the boys who had been at the talk had been caught out on a hill in a storm and had died from exposure. He had been found buried in a snowdrift with his right hand clasping his left ring finger. All those who found him were puzzled. In a desperate attempt to understand what it meant they decided to phone the preacher in the vain hope that he could explain.

As the preacher told them of Psalm 23 and his talk just a few days before, he said 'I know where that boy is now. He is in heaven. As that boy held his finger he was able to say 'The Lord is MY shepherd'. And if he could say that, so he was also able to say the words with which the psalm ends, 'And I will dwell in the house of the Lord forever.'

It is a terribly moving story. But what was said of that boy can be said by any true Christian. Whatever happens and however we die, we can know for sure that we will dwell in the house of the Lord for ever if we turn to him and know that great shepherd as our own.

A_New_Heaven and_a_New Earth

III

What_about_other_faiths?

We live in a world of easy communication and travel. Different countries and the beliefs of those who live in them are no longer shrouded in the mystery with which they were once associated. And therefore in the minds of many the edges of culture and belief have been blurred. People are people, it is argued. They believe what they believe because of the history and geography of the place where they were born. Who are we to say who is right and who is wrong? As a result, in western countries it is now seen as an offence to claim that anything is absolute, let alone true. Professor Allan Bloom began his book *The Closing of the American Mind* with these words:

'There is one thing a professor can be absolutely certain of: almost every student entering the university believes, or says he believes, that truth is relative.'[116]

Inevitably these ideas seep through into everyday thinking. How can we claim that Jesus is the only way when there are so many people with different faiths, many of whom may have never heard about Jesus? Surely, different faiths are no more than different roads up the same mountain, different ways of speaking about the same God, different aspects of the same truth or equally valid truths? School text books enshrine the assumption that 'members of different faiths [are] fellow pilgrims following different paths through life in the same search for truth and happiness.'[117] And we are all left thinking that it is an offence and offensive to make any claim to absolute truth.

Whilst such concerns might be understandable, they are neither logical nor Christian. It might be appealing to believe that all the faiths are the same, or that all truth is relative, but adherents to almost all of the world's belief systems would disagree.

WESTERN_ARROGANCE

A friend of mine was having a social meeting with a Muslim. They had met to talk about their faiths and how they differed. The Muslim began the conversation by saying, 'I think you are going to hell. You think I am going to hell. We can't both be right.' Although the language is strong and shocking, it does reveal a reality about different faiths – namely that they are not all the same. A Christian believes Jesus is the Son of God. A Muslim does not. A Hindu believes that there are many gods – a Christian does not.

If we are to say that all religions are the same then we are claiming one of two things about God. Either we know more about God than the different world faiths – so much so that it is possible for *us* to claim that they really believe in the same thing although *they* do not recognize it. Or we are claiming that God is so unknowable that it is possible to say almost anything about him without anyone or anything refuting our assertions. Either way, we would be making hugely arrogant claims without having any authority but our own to make such statements. And if our statements are true then *we* become the ultimate source of revelation and knowledge of God.

Of course, people never assume that they are setting themselves up as an authority. It is seen as tolerance and understanding. It is considered a virtue to escape from the tyranny of the absolute – but it becomes the height of arrogance, both because it is the only absolute statement which is allowed and also because it claims an ultimate authority which it denies to any other belief system. Far better to be honest – to make the point that different religions do not all believe the same thing, that it is possible for them all to be wrong, but impossible for them all to be right.

Sincerity_does_not_mean_truth

It is possible for people to be very sincere about what they believe but to be sincerely wrong. When I was young a friend of mine was convinced that Father Christmas existed. He said that he had seen him. Only years later was he told that one Christmas his father had hired a costume, come into his bedroom and filled his stocking. What he had seen was not Santa at all, but his Dad. My friend, although young, was absolutely sincere in his belief. But he was sincerely wrong.

I have no doubt that anyone who takes their religion seriously is sincere about what they believe. But that sincerity does not mean that they are right. Truth should not be based on what people believe, but belief should be based on what is true. And therefore the question which we must ask is quite simply that: 'what is true?'

Jesus said 'I am the way, the truth and the life. No one comes to the father except through me.'[118] That is an absolute statement. It is therefore true or false. Either Jesus is the only way to God and all other beliefs are wrong, or he is not the way to God and Christians are in serious error. What we cannot say is that someone who sincerely believes that Jesus was not who he said he was is in the same position as someone who sincerely believes that he was. They are both sincere, but they are not both right. We must decide.

But here you might raise the objection about those who live in other countries and who are brought up with another faith. It seems wrong to 'impose' the Christian faith on those people and cultures who are content, happy and settled in what they believe. It is argued that the Christian cause has been the root of conflict and hatred in the world, not harmony and forgiveness and peace.

Certainly no one looking at the history of the church or the world could fail to realize that many wrongs have been done to culture and people in the so-called name of Christianity. Undoubtedly missionaries over the years have made mistakes. Culture has been brought rather than the gospel — western ideology has been taught rather than Christ. But it must be remembered that the gospel is different. It will bring with it a culture, but a culture defined by Jesus, not a western mindset. That counter-cultural community was first seen, not in an educated white culture, but in an occupied Middle Eastern culture. The only reason we have the Christian faith in the West is because of missionary endeavour in the past from the East.

The message of the gospel is for all. And we are all born as those who have not heard and do not know. There may be obstacles which prevent us hearing or make it difficult for those who seek to tell us to reach us, but fundamentally we are all in the same boat. For some, the misunderstandings of the Christian faith given to them in a so-called Christian country such as Britain can be as much a barrier (social and otherwise) as the entirely different belief system of another country.

The gospel will disturb. It will disturb the white middle class Caucasian who has adopted a comfortable 'churchianity' devoid of Christ. And it will disturb the Middle Eastern Muslim who is embedded in Islamic culture. But if it is true, it is true and however sincerely we hold to another belief, we would be sincerely wrong.

Ironically, those of other faiths would say the same about what they believe. Islam is a missionary faith. It seeks converts. It would not be so established in countries which were once Christian if it did not. Others too want their faith to be known. But we can't all be right. It boils down to what is true and how those who hold on to that truth deal with others. Sincerity is important. But not sincerity without truth.

PART_III

WHAT_NOW?

WHAT_NOW?

As I have spoken to people about the Christian faith, I have often had the response 'I never knew.' There has simply been a lack of understanding about what the Christian faith is and therefore what it means to be a Christian. All those I have known who have looked seriously at the claims of Christ and the truth of the gospel have decided that it is true. All who have had the courage to enquire have been struck by the coherence, reliability and historicity of Jesus. But most have not responded to his offer of forgiveness and new life. And that is because the Christian faith is not just a matter of intellectual assent. If I were to describe a chair to a person who had never seen one before, I might be able to convince them that it will hold their weight. In other words, they might believe what I say. But it is not until they sit on the chair that faith is being exercised.

So it is with the Christian faith. You might believe that Jesus was who he said he was. But that is a world away from having faith in Christ. One is intellectual assent; the other is a life changing decision. If you decide to follow Christ, it will involve a new set of priorities, a new perspective and a concern not to live for yourself but for the one who made you and rescued you. You will be misunderstood and sometimes isolated. You will be light in a world that prefers darkness and you will make statements about truth in a world which is riddled with lies. But you will also experience joy and peace, the delight of a new relationship with God and with other Christians. And most importantly of all you will have the glorious guarantee of heaven.

Sometimes I have been asked how someone becomes a Christian, as if there is a magic formula. There is not. My baptism and, if I am Anglican, my confirmation, do not make me a Christian. God makes me a Christian through the work of Christ. And as I respond to his message in repentance and faith I begin a new life with him — that is the Christian life. I will want to read the Bible, so that I can learn how to please him. I will want to pray, so that I can talk to him. I will want to meet with other Christians so that I can encourage them and be encouraged by them. And I will want to live to please him.

That new life begins as I recognize my rebellion against God and ask his forgiveness, a forgiveness which is only possible because of the death of Jesus on the cross. I will need the help of his Spirit so that I can live that new life with Jesus as my ruler.

Some Christians can look back to a particular moment when they made a decision to follow Christ, others will have gradually realized that they do believe and accept the substitutional death of Jesus and his Lordship over their lives.

What is important is that whether by a process or at a particular point of time, we come under the Lordship of Christ by virtue of his death for us.

It might be that the following prayer will help you to make that response so that you can begin the Christian life:

> Dear God, I recognize that I have rebelled against you
> and that I am not worthy to be accepted by you.
> I thank you that you sent Jesus Christ into the world to
> die on a cross so that I can be forgiven.
> Thank you that in his resurrection there is certainty
> of new life under his Lordship.
> Please forgive me and change me by your Spirit, that
> I might live with Jesus as my ruler.
>   AMEN

If you have made a commitment to Jesus, then tell someone. We all need to be part of a living, learning fellowship of Christians. Others will help and encourage you. Above all, you will have begun the most wonderful and exciting life this side of heaven, with the joy and wonder of a relationship with the living God and the glory of heaven beyond. From having nothing, you now have everything.

NOTES

1 *Time*, 30 March 1992

2 Bernard Levin, quoted in *Questions of Life* Nicky Gumbel.
   (Eastbourne: Kingsway 1994) ,p.14

3 Douglas Coupland *Life After God* (Touchstone 1994),p359

4 Isaiah 40:25, 26

5 Psalm 96:13

6 Exodus 20:3

7 John 1:11-13

8 C. F. Vonwezacher

9 The late Donald Mackay, Professor of Communications and
   Neuroscience

10 Professor W. R. Thompson

11 Sir Hermann Bandi (Cosmologist)

12 Professor Chanra Wickeramansinge (Astronomer)

13 Gordon Wenham *Genesis 1-15* (WORD UK, 1991) p.xiv

14 Psalm 90:4

15 Wenham, *Genesis,* p.39

16 Genesis 1:14

17 Genesis 1:31

18 *The Times* 20 September 1999

19 Craig L.Blomberg *Neither Poverty nor Riches* (Leicester:Apollos
   1999) p.18

20 Genesis 2:16-17

21 Genesis 3:1b

22 Genesis 3:2-3

23 Genesis 3:4

24 Lord Winston. BBC1 17 June 1998

25 Romans 3:23

[26] 2 Corinthians 8:9

[27] Quoted in J.R.W. Stott *The Cross of Christ.*(Leicester: IVP 1986)

[28] ibid p.23,24

[29] Revelation 21:4

[30] 2 Corinthians 11:23-27

[31] 2 Corinthians 12:9

[32] Quoted in David Pawson *The Road to Hell* (London: Hodder and Stoughton) p.15 Written by a journalist in the 1960s

[33] C.S. Lewis *The Problem of Pain* (London: Fount 1940 p.94,95

[34] D.A.Carson *The Gagging of God* (Leicester: Apollos 1996) p.521

[35] Matthew 25:46

[36] Matthew 10:28

[37] Luke 16:26

[38] J.R.W. Stott *Christian Mission in the Modern World* (Leicester: IVP 1975) p.113

[39] C.S. Lewis *The Problem of Pain*, (Fount, 1986) p.98

[40] ibid.

[41] Peter Jensen *At the Heart of the Universe* (Leicester:IVP 1991) p.32

[42] 1 Timothy 1:15

[43] Romans 3:9-11

[44] Acts 17:31

[45] Matthew 28:19

[46] Paul Barnett *Is the New Testament History?* (London: Hodder and Stoughton) p.9

[47] 'An audience with Spike Milligan' ITV February 1996

[48] J.R.W.Stott *Basic Christianity* (Leicester: IVP 1958) p.21

[49] Mark 1:15

[50] C.S. Lewis *Mere Christianity* (London: Fontana 1985) p.52

51 Mark 2:7

52 John 8:58

53 Exodus 3:14

54 John 14:9

55 Matthew 1:1

56 2 Samuel 7:12-16

57 Genesis 12:2,3

58 John 5:39-41

59 Luke 24:25-27

60 Matthew 5:44

61 Luke 23:34

62 1 Peter 2:22

63 J.R.W. Stott *The Cross of Christ* p.17-19

64 Galatians 6:14

65 1 Corinthians 2:2

66 Matthew 27:41-51a

67 2 Corinthians 5:19

68 Amos 8:9

69 Matthew 11:27

70 John 3:16

71 R.T. France *Evidence relating to Jesus* (London: Hodder and Stoughton, 1986) p.20

72 Tacitus, *Annals* 15:44

73 Suetonius, *Claudius* 25:4

74 Josephus *Antiquities* 18:63,64

75 Josephus, *Antiquities* 20:200

76 J.R.W. Stott *The Cross of Christ* p.25

77 C.Blomberg *The Historical Reliability of the Gospels* (Leicester: IVP 1987) p.240

[78] ibid. p.257

[79] Luke 24:18-24

[80] Luke 24:25-27

[81] 2 Timothy 3:15

[82] Matthew 28:20

[83] 2 Timothy 1:13; 2:2

[84] Ephesians 1:1

[85] 1 Corinthians 15:17

[86] G.E. Ladd *I Believe in the Resurrection of Jesus* (London: Hodder and Stoughton 1975) p.42

[87] Mark 8:31

[88] Acts 2:31

[89] John 19:41

[90] Matthew 28:11-15

[91] Quoted in *The Making of Modern German Christology* A.E.McGrath

[92] Acts 2:36

[93] F. Morrison *Who Moved the Stone?* (London: Faber)

[94] Romans 6:23

[95] 2 Timothy 2:8

[96] 2 Samuel 7:16

[97] Ephesians 1:22

[98] Acts 17:31

[99] John 14:16,17

[100] Romans 8:15-17a

[101] 1 John 3:1

[102] John 13:34,35

[103] Quoted in 'Christianity Explored' Leaders manual, Rico Tice (London:Paternoster) p.172

[104] Information taken from *Why they can't believe?* Paul Weston, Frameworks, p.55

[105] *The Sheep that got away* (MARC, Monarch Publications, 1993) p.28

[106] Philippians 2:6-8

[107] Revelation 21:4

[108] Genesis 1:31

[109] Revelation 21:27

[110] Revelation 5:9

[111] Revelation 5:5

[112] Revelation 5:6

[113] Ephesians 1:14

[114] 2 Corinthians 5:1-5

[115] Taken from *A Call to Spiritual Reformation* D.A.Carson (Downers Grove, Illinois: IVP, 1992) p.62

[116] Allan Bloom *The Closing of The American Mind.* (London: Penguin, 1988) p.25

[117] James Taylor and Jan Thompson *The Christian Story* (London: Hodder and Stoughton) p.76

[118] John 14:6

Christian Focus Publications publishes biblically-accurate books for adults and children. The books in the adult range are published in three imprints.

Christian Heritage contains classic writings from the past.

Christian Focus contains popular works including biographies, commentaries, doctrine, and Christian living.

Mentor focuses on books written at a level suitable for Bible College and seminary students, pastors, and others; the imprint includes commentaries, doctrinal studies, examination of current issues, and church history.

For a free catalogue of all our titles, please write to

Christian Focus Publications, Ltd.
Geanies House, Fearn, Tain,
Ross-shire, IV20 1TW, Great Britain

For details of our titles visit us on our web site

http://www.christianfocus.com